AIR CAMPAIGN

SIX-DAY WAR 1967

Operation *Focus* and the 12 hours that changed the Middle East

SHLOMO ALONI ILLUSTRATED BY ADAM TOOBY

OSPREY PUBLISHING
Bloomsbury Publishing Plc
PO Box 883, Oxford, OX1 9PL, UK
1385 Broadway, 5th Floor, New York, NY 10018, USA
E-mail: info@ospreypublishing.com
www.ospreypublishing.com

OSPREY is a trademark of Osprey Publishing Ltd

First published in Great Britain in 2019

A catalog record for this book is available from the British Library.

ISBN: PB 9781472835277; eBook 9781472835284;
ePDF 9781472835291; XML 9781472835307

19 20 21 22 23   10 9 8 7 6 5 4 3 2 1

Maps by Bounford.com
3D BEV by Paul Kime
Diagrams by Adam Tooby
Index by Zoe Ross
Typeset by PDQ Digital Media Solutions, Bungay, UK
Printed in China through World Print Ltd

Osprey Publishing supports the Woodland Trust, the UK's leading woodland conservation
charity.

To find out more about our authors and books visit www.ospreypublishing.com. Here
you will find extracts, author interviews, details of forthcoming events and the option to
sign up for our newsletter.

Acknowledgments

This book is a humble tribute to Israel Air Force flyers from the era of the June 1967
Six-Day War, dozens of whom have contributed to the ongoing research that yielded this
text. Special thanks to IAF veterans; to colleagues and friends, foremost among them
modeling maestro Asher Roth and BIAF editor Yehuda Borovik; to ILGOV Defense
Archive staff, from Micha and BatSheva via Doron and Shirli to Ifat and Efrat, as well as
Avi and Goel; to ILGOV Premiere Press Office; to IDF Censorship.
The formal military-style presentation of [rank] [name] was rejected in favor of the less formal
[name] only presentation in order to save space as well as to avoid confusion and repetition.
IAF codes for radio callsigns were translated from Hebrew to English in order to ease
reading and are presented in capital letters.
Terminology used in this text for military units is [type] [number] in line with proper
presentation in Hebrew as well as in Arabic.
IAF names for aircraft and systems were not translated into English but presented in
English as pronounced in Hebrew.
The events are presented along a timeline. There are actually two timelines: the timeline
of departures and that of actions. Departure times are supposedly accurate; action times
are mostly approximated.
Despite all best efforts, when writing about history errors and omissions are inevitable.
Apologies.
Shlomo Aloni
25 September 2018

Times

All times presented in this text are
Israel local time which was, during the
summer of 1967, two hours later than
Greenwich Mean Time and one hour
earlier than Egypt local time (the conflict
taking place during summer time in
Egypt): for example, 0905hrs Israel time
was 0705hrs GMT and 1005hrs Egypt
local time.

Abbreviations

AC: Author's collection
ARC: Asher Roth Collection
EAF: Egyptian Air Force
IAF: Israel Air Force. In Israel the IDF
Chief of Staff is the supreme commander
of the armed forces; Israel Air Force is an
arm of IDF and the IAF Commander is
subordinated to the IDF Chief of Staff
AIR3 was Operations Branch, the third
branch of the IAF Air Department;
the other two IAF staff departments
were Adjutancy and Material; the other
branches of the Air Department
during the summer of 1967 were:
AIR1 Organization,
AIR2 Weapon Systems, AIR4 Intelligence,
AIR5 Training and AIR6 Control
IDF: Israel Defense Force
ILGD/A: Israel Government Defense/
Archive
ILGP/PO: Israel Government Premiere/
Press Office
JAF: Jordanian Air Force
SAF: Syrian Air Force

CONTENTS

INTRODUCTION

Four years after the Arab world's first attempt to annihilate Israel, Egypt – the leader of Arab nations and Israel's prime opponent at the time – became a republic on July 23, 1952. Gamal Abdel Nasser, its new socialist, pan-Arabist leader, pursued a policy of seeking unification with ideologically like-minded Arab states, chiefly Syria. The United States, fearing Soviet influence in the Middle East, launched an initiative – codenamed Alpha – to support Egypt politically, economically and militarily, conditional upon a peace agreement with Israel.

In June 1955, Nasser attempted to break the linkage between US aid and peace with Israel. Nasser spoke of his discouragement over the previous three years that military equipment could be obtained from the US. He had concluded that he should accept Russia's offer of military equipment.

On September 21, 1955, Nasser notified the US that the arms deal between Czechoslovakia and Egypt for Soviet weapons was to go ahead. Two days later, the US indicated that the deal included 200 jet aircraft, of which 100 – comprising 37 medium jet bombers and the remainder MiG-15s – were to be delivered by December 1955, with first shipment already on its way to Egypt.

Nasser stated that the Czechoslovak arms deal was a turning point in Egyptian history. Israel reasoned that, given Nasser's intentions of Arab unity and Egypt's new capability of offensive bombers, Egypt was seeking a second-round war to eliminate the disgrace of defeat in the 1948 war, as well as to remove the geographical buffer that Israel represented between Egypt in Africa and the majority of Arab nations in Asia.

Then, on July 26, 1956, Nasser nationalized the Suez Canal. France and Britain combined forces to repossess the Suez Canal, and Israel joined the coalition. The resulting 1956 war ended in mixed results for all four participants. France and UK defeated Egypt militarily, but did not repossess the Suez Canal and were forced to retreat by political pressure. Egypt was beaten, but scored a diplomatic victory and Nasser's regime survived. Israel destroyed Egypt's war machine, yet was forced to retreat from Sinai – but only after securing American

5

Israeli troops examine Egyptian coastal artillery – most likely disabled by the Egyptian crew through double-loading it and then firing it prior to the Egyptian retreat from Ras Nasrani in November 1956 – in early 1957, with the Straits of Tiran in the background. (ILGP/PO)

assurances over freedom of navigation in the Straits of Tiran. A few days prior to their withdrawal, Israel's Foreign Minister in the UN General Assembly and the Prime Minister in the Israeli Parliament both stated solemnly that any interference with Israel's freedom of navigation through the Straits of Tiran would be regarded as an attack, entitling Israel to exercise its right to self-defense.

Egypt rehabilitated its armed forces and reinstated the policy of Arab unity more intensely than ever before. Egypt and Syria became the United Arab Republic on February 22, 1958, with tiny Israel forming a buffer between the south and north of the gargantuan

Israel's Prime Minister and Defense Minister Levy Eshkol, center, examining, on April 8, 1967, Syrian artillery bombardment damage to housing at Gadot, with IDF Chief of Staff Isaac Rabin, left, and Command North Commander David Elazar, right. (ILGP/PO)

conglomeration. The United Arab Republic dissolved on September 28, 1961, but almost exactly a year later, on September 26, 1962, Nasser embarked upon another Arab unity venture with an Egyptian-sponsored rebellion in Yemen.

On June 10, 1964, Israel's inauguration of the National Pipeline that streamed water from the Sea of Galilee to irrigate the Negev Desert was a major milestone in a dispute concerning regional resources of water that evolved into the Water War: a series of occasional armed clashes, mostly between Israel and Syria.

The clashes between Israel and Syria tested Nasser's rhetoric concerning Arab solidarity at a time when Egypt was deeply involved in Yemen and not yet ready, militarily, to confront Israel. In the wake of a major clash between Israel and Syria on April 7, 1967, tension along the Israeli-Syrian border remained high, but the IDF did not evaluate the situation as volatile. American analysis of the situation in the Middle East also seemed to rule out the potential for full-scale war. A memo of May 1, 1967 from the American Undersecretary of State to the President stated:

> Israel has a safe margin of superiority over any combination of Arab forces likely to attack it and can be expected to maintain that position for at least the next five years. Arab numerical

All six former IDF Chiefs inspected the two IDF decisive forces – air force and armor corps – on May 16, 1967. This visit had been arranged before the start of the crisis, which was then not seen as exceptional. Here, left to right, are: Jacob Dori, IDF Chief 1948–49; IAF Commander Moti Hod; Khatsor Wing 4 Commander Beni Peled; Squadron 101 Commander Amos Lapidot; IDF Chief Isaac Rabin; and Moshe Dayan, Defense Minister from June 2, 1967. (AC)

The IAF mobilized a total of 10,983 reservists from May 18 to 26, 1967. Photographed at Khatsor during the Waiting Period, Squadron 105 reservists play backgammon, massage, and read. Their Super Mystère, parked at a dispersal point because the IAF ran out of hardened aircraft shelters (HAS) owing to the constant improvements in serviceability during the crisis, is armed and ready to fight. (AC)

force superiority is more than matched by Israel's superiority in training, leadership, military doctrine and maintenance of equipment. Moreover, the Arab states have made little progress in military coordination among themselves. Recent border clashes have demonstrated that short of general hostilities, or Israeli occupation of Arab territory, the Arab states will not rush to one another's assistance.

The IDF General Staff Branch Chief, Ezer Weizman, addressed the Israeli public on May 4, 1967, prior to Israel's Independence Day, to explain the IDF's evaluation that no major war between Israel and an Arab nation was expected during the following year, though more border clashes with Syria seemed likely.

A series of small-scale terrorist attacks against Israeli infrastructure, traffic, and settlements started on May 5, 1967, and Israel held Syria responsible. A reprisal operation seemed inevitable. Syria responded to the accusations with claims that Israel was planning a large-scale attack and plotting to overthrow the Syrian government. Although the IDF believed that Arab solidarity was shaky, Syria claimed that the Egypt-Syria mutual defense treaty, signed on November 4, 1966, would be implemented if Israel attacked. Possibly in an attempt to assess Israeli preparedness for an attack, a Syrian reconnaissance mission was flown over northern Israel, west of the Israeli-Syrian border, on May 14, 1967. Regardless of the evolving crisis, Israel resolved to stage its Independence Day military parade in Jerusalem planned for the next day.

Apparently in response to the war of words, and possibly as a result of the Syrian reconnaissance flight, the Egyptian Army started to roll forward, into Sinai, towards the Egyptian-Israeli border. Was it merely coincidence that the Israeli Prime Minister was notified that the Egyptian armed forces were marching across the Suez Canal into the Sinai Peninsula while he was in Jerusalem reviewing the IDF's Independence Day parade? The IDF's belief that Arab solidarity was shaky had been shattered, and its evaluation that war against an Arab nation should not be expected in the coming year was being tested.

Did Nasser consider war when he ordered his forces to advance into Sinai? Israel viewed Egypt's deployment of forces to Sinai as a dramatic act aimed at deterring Israel from attacking

Syria. But since Israel had no immediate intention to do so, the crisis initially looked like an ostentatious Egyptian show of force, primarily aimed at reviving the pan-Arab solidarity that the IDF had evaluated only weeks before as practically nonexistent.

Then Nasser began a series of acts that changed the course of events. Egypt demanded the withdrawal of the United Nations Emergency Force (UNEF), a buffer force of observers deployed between Egypt and Israel in Sinai; their withdrawal was confirmed on May 17, 1967. The situation no longer looked like an empty act of Arab solidarity in a war of words between Israel and Syria, but as a real danger. The IAF suspended training on May 18, mobilized reserves and was ready for war from May 19.

In an attempt to cool down the regional heat, the Israeli Prime Minister stated on May 22:

> From this stand I would like to repeat and say to Arab nations, including Egypt and Syria that we are not heading for attack. We have no interest to interfere with their security, territory or legitimate rights. We will not interfere in their internal affairs, in their regimes, in their regional and international relationships. We claim, in line with the principle of mutuality, to apply the same principles towards us.

Israeli Prime Minister Levy Eshkol addressing the Israeli Parliament, the Knesset, on May 22, 1967, with David Ben-Gurion first from left in the second row and Moshe Dayan – who is not yet a minister and therefore not sitting in the first row – to his left. (ILGP/PO)

> During the first days of the Egyptian armed forces deployment in Sinai, there were nations that viewed this deployment as a demonstrative action without military implications. Others can accept such interpretations but since this deployment is close to our border, it is our opinion that we must take all precautionary steps against any possible development. Due to Egyptian deployment along the border and the withdrawal of UNEF, I ordered a limited mobilization of reserve forces that had already been completed.

> After completion of limited mobilization of reserves, I visited the IDF. The magnificent quality of our armed forces that was fostered and perfected over many years has reached a high standard. The IDF can now face any test with the same devotion and talent that it had demonstrated in the past and even more.

Egyptian President Gamal Abdel Nasser during his visit to an EAF base on May 22, 1967. (AC)

To end with, I call on the region's nations for mutual respect of sovereignty, entirety, and international rights of every nation. Israel, fully confident in its power and spirit, is expressing its willingness to take part in an effort to bring quiet and peace to our region.

The Egyptian President's fiery response to this speech followed after midnight, May 23, when Nasser announced the closure of the Straits of Tiran to Israeli shipping. In his speech, Nasser claimed that he ordered, on May 14, the deployment of Egyptian forces to Sinai in light of information that Israel was amassing 13 brigades along the Israeli-Syrian border,[1] and stated that, "[The coming] war will be an opportunity for Israel to realize that whatever was written about [Israel's] occupation of Sinai in 1956 was fabricated." Adding insult to injury, Nasser, laughing and mocking with Egyptian Air Force (EAF) fighter pilots, made an immortal statement: "They [Israel] threaten war and we tell them 'Ahalan VaSahalan' (welcome)."

Israel turned to the United States to enforce its 1957 guarantee of freedom of navigation through the Straits of Tiran, but to no avail. For all practical purposes, Nasser's speech, as broadcast on May 23, made war in the Middle East inevitable.

1   The IDF regular order of battle was much smaller than 13 brigades, and even with full mobilization of reserves the IDF's front-line force numbered nine armored brigades, four infantry brigades and three para brigades for a total of 16 brigades, so it would have been unlikely for the IDF to deploy 13 brigades for a Command North action against Syria with a balance of only three brigades for Command Center to face Jordan, Command South to face Egypt and the IDF reserve to face unexpected eventualities; in any case, there was no large-scale mobilization of IDF reserves at that time, so even such a remote scenario was impossible at the time and points to poor practice by Egyptian intelligence or deliberate inflation on the part of Egypt's President.

CHRONOLOGY

1967

March 16 IAF AIR3 distributes Operation Plan 67/11 *Focus* with an objective to accomplish air superiority through suppression of enemy airfields and destruction of enemy aircraft.

April 7 Israel and Syria clash in the air; Israel claims the downing of six Syrian MiG-21s while Syria indirectly admitted the loss of at least four MiG-21s.

April 10 EAF Commander visits Syria, probably to learn lessons from the April 7 clash and to evaluate the situation.

April 10 IAF Commander Moti Hod promoted from colonel to major general.

April 15 Syria issues plan for Operation *Nasser* with an objective to invade Israel and occupy a sector of Galilee; the plan for the Syrian Air Force (SAF)'s Division 3 and Division 7 is to support the Syrian Army's Division 12 and Division 35.

April 17 Syrian President states that Syria will continue to support Palestinian actions against Israel.

April 18 Egyptian Prime Minister begins a visit to Syria; prior to his arrival, his Syrian counterpart states that an Israeli offensive against Syria is imminent.

April 30 IAF Squadron 110 Vautours photograph inside Syria, east of the Israeli-Syrian border.

May 4 IDF General Staff Branch Chief Ezer Weizman – formerly IAF Commander from 1958 to 1966 – indicates IDF evaluation that no major war between Israel and an Arab nation is expected during the following year, though more border clashes with Syria seem a likely possibility.

May 9 Israeli Foreign Minister warns Syria that Israel will not tolerate Syrian-sponsored terror attacks without reaction.

May 11–13 EAF bomb inside Saudi Arabia in retaliation for Saudi sponsorship of Royalist rebels in Yemen.

May 13 Israeli Prime Minister warns Syria that Israel will react against terrorist attacks and against nations that host terrorists.

May 14 SAF conducts a mission – possibly visual reconnaissance – over Israel, west of the Israeli-Syrian border, probably to examine if Israel is amassing forces in order to attack Syria.

May 14 Egyptian President orders land forces to deploy forward into Sinai Peninsula, possibly in order to deter Israel from attacking Syria.

May 15 Israel's Independence Day military march in Jerusalem coincides with reports about the deployment of Egyptian forces into Sinai.

May 16, 0905hrs IDF activates Plan *Rogel*, the contingency plan for the defense of Israel, in response to Egypt's actions.

May 16, 1905hrs IDF authorizes mobilization of Brigade 520 as a precautionary step in light of the Egyptian deployment in Sinai.

May 17, 0600hrs Egypt orders UNEF to withdraw from Sinai; the head of Egypt's armed forces states that they have been ordered to prepare for action against Israel should Israel attack any Arab state, while the armed forces of Jordan and Syria step up readiness.

IAF Mirages and SAF MiG-21s clashed in four air combats on April 7. The IAF claimed six air-to-air kills and released six Mirage gunsight films to back this claim; the black wedges at top left indicate if the trigger was pressed at the time. Syria admitted to losing four MiGs; if true, the IAF over-claim was 150 percent, which compares well with the Syrian "infinite over-claim" of four kills against true IAF losses of nil. (AC)

The IAF's contribution to the IDF military march in Jerusalem during Israel Independence Day on May 15, 1967, was limited to a few AAA guns as the parade was austere and modest – and did not include an IAF flyover – so that Israel would comply with armistice limitations. Three days later, the reserve bulk of the IAF's AAA force was mobilized to defend IAF bases from a potential Egyptian offensive. (ILGP/PO)

May 17, 1600hrs EAF MiG-21s – flying fast and high – conduct a mission of unknown nature (IAF evaluates that EAF MiG-21s are not fit for photography under such flight parameters and Egypt never releases photos) across the Negev, flying from Jordan to Egypt including over Dimona.

May 17, 1730hrs – in light of the two escalating Egyptian actions earlier that day – IAF orders suspension of training and step-up of readiness, with Squadron 119 deploying Mirages to Khatserim and IDF mobilizing Brigade 200.

May 17, 2330hrs IDF orders Readiness Level C; the highest readiness state.

May 18 EAF issues Battle Order 67/3 with the objective to support an Egyptian offensive aimed at occupation of the Negev's southern sector.

May 18 IAF initiates mobilization of reserves, at first to bolster defense and from May 20 to enable an offensive option while also starting to implement deployment in line with prior planning for war, including relocation of Squadron 107 from Ramat David to Lod on May 19.

May 19 EAF issues Battle Order 67/2 with the objective to strike IAF bases in order to accomplish air superiority. The order defines a turnaround timeframe of 175 minutes.

May 20 Iraq's Deputy Prime Minister arrives in Egypt in order to evaluate how Iraq can militarily support Egypt.

May 23, 0345hrs IDF Intelligence informs the IDF Chief that Egypt has blocked the Straits of Tiran to Israeli shipping. Earlier that night, Egypt radio broadcasts a recorded speech in which Egyptian President announces the blockade and states that Israel is threatening war, but tells them "Ahalan VaSahalan" (welcome).

May 23, 1320hrs IDF General Staff convenes to discuss the new situation and authorizes mobilization of eight brigades.

May 23, 1630hrs IDF General Staff convenes for presentation of Operation *Focus* plan.

May 24, 1030hrs IDF General Staff convenes for discussion of Operation *Red Tongue*, a deception plan

Prime Minister and Defense Minister Levy Eshkol – left, wearing a beret – visited IDF Command South on May 25, two days after Israel began mobilizing the bulk of IDF reserves. Alongside Eshkol are, right to left: Deputy Prime Minister Yigael Alon (who was, in 1948, IDF Front D Commander, the forerunner of IDF Command South); IDF Chief of Staff Yitzhak Rabin; and IDF Command South Chief Isaiah Gavish. (ILGP/PO)

aimed at luring Egypt into believing that the IDF is preparing for an offensive against Sharm El Sheikh at the southern tip of Sinai in order to open the Straits of Tiran. Later that day, IAF Vautours fly a reconnaissance mission over Sharm El Sheikh in line with *Red Tongue*.

May 24, 1730hrs IDF General Staff presents to Israeli Prime Minister the two preferred plans: IAF Operation *Focus*, aimed at destruction of the EAF, and IDF Operation *Axe 2*, aimed at destruction of the Egyptian Army in northern Sinai.

May 26 EAF MiG-21s again fly over Dimona, this time flying east from Sinai, turning around Dimona and returning west to Sinai. IAF Mirages are scrambled but are unable to catch the trespassers. The objective of the flight is again unknown, as IAF evaluation is that EAF MiG-21s are not fit for photography from high altitude at high speed.

May 30 President Nasser and King Hussein signed – in Cairo, on May 30, 1967 – a mutual defense treaty that tightened the ring round Israel, placed Jordanian armed forces under Egyptian command, and enabled Egypt to deploy forces to Jordan.

June 1 A new Israeli Government is formed and enters office the following day, with Moshe Dayan taking over from Prime Minister Levy Eshkol as Defense Minister. Stalemate plays into Arab hands because of the negative impact of IDF mobilization of reserves upon the Israeli economy. The new harder-line Israeli Government is a signal to the world that Israel will not tolerate the situation for much longer.

June 3 Israel concludes, from letter by USA President to Israeli Prime Minister, that diplomatic efforts to force Egypt to withdraw forces from Sinai and lift the blockade at the Straits of Tiran have practically failed. Certain conducts in USA diplomatic messages to Israel could be interpreted as a green light for Israel to attack Egypt.

June 4 Iraq joins the Egyptian-Jordanian mutual defense treaty, with Iraqi troops deployed to Egypt and Jordan, while the Iraqi delegation that signed the treaty in Cairo is due to visit Jordan on its way back from Egypt to Iraq on June 5. Nasser states that an international initiative to lift the maritime blockade at the Straits of Tiran will be viewed by Egypt as an intervention in internal affairs and an act of war against Egypt. Egyptian President again welcomes Israel to attack Egypt so that the whole world will witness the military might of Egypt, unlike in 1956 when Israel waged war against Egypt under the patronage of France and UK.

June 4, 0830hrs the Israeli Government convenes and subsequently authorizes the IDF to attack Egypt in order to suppress the EAF, destroy the Egyptian Army in Sinai and lift the Egyptian blockade at the Straits of Tiran.

By the spring of 1967, IAF combat aircraft squadrons operated from HAS, plus a quick-reaction alert (QRA) complex closer to the squadron headquarters and the runway threshold. This was a sun shelter with four cells for two QRA pairs, while a spare aircraft was parked beside the sun shelter, as in this view of the Squadron 101 QRA complex at Khatsor in April 1967. (AC)

ATTACKER'S CAPABILITIES
197 jets that changed the Middle East

Air superiority has been a cornerstone of Israel's defense doctrine ever since the IAF's inception. The IAF's first-ever fighter operation plan was to strike the EAF's El Arish air base with five Avia S-199s, the Czechoslovak version of the German Messerschmitt Bf 109 and the IAF's first fighter type. This debut fighter operation had to be canceled after Egyptian forces were spotted south of Tel Aviv, and the four available S-199s were scrambled to strike them instead. However, the IAF's desire for air superiority was quickly engraved in its heritage. On July 29, 1948, Israel's first Prime Minister and Defense Minister David Ben Gurion defined the IAF's missions, with air superiority officially graded as the IAF's priority:

1. The main mission is the complete destruction of the enemy's air power in the air or on the ground
2. Tactical support of ground and naval forces
3. Destruction of strategic targets

Ten years later, on July 25, 1958, Ezer Weizman entered office as IAF Commander. By then the IAF had been preparing for an air superiority campaign for almost a decade, and had actually witnessed such a campaign in 1956 when Anglo-French forces attacked Egypt. Although the EAF was successfully suppressed, the Anglo-French operational concept – suppress enemy airfields during nighttime with strategic bombers and destroy enemy aircraft during daytime with tactical fighters – was not one the IAF was equipped to adopt.

1960s operational concepts

The IAF's ingenious counter-concept, one better suited to its fleet of fighter and attack aircraft, was to combine suppression with destruction. The raiders would first bomb runways and then turn back to strafe the immobile aircraft. A single four-ship formation, flying one bombing run and three strafing passes, could, potentially, suppress one runway or two intersecting runways as well as destroying up to 12 enemy aircraft. Lacking a sufficient order

The IAF fighter force consisted entirely of French aircraft. Here, in July 1965, a Vautour leads an Ouragan and a Fouga armed trainer, with a Super Mystère, Mirage, and Mystère behind. After 1967, it sought a new light attack aircraft (A-4 Skyhawk) and a heavy attack aircraft (F-4 Phantom) to complement the modern Mirage air-to-air combat aircraft. (AC)

Ezer Weizman was one of the five pilots assigned to the IAF's first planned fighter raid on El Arish in May 1948. An RAF-trained fighter pilot, Weizman would become IAF Commander from 1958 until 1966, when this photo was taken in the cockpit of his famous Black Spitfire. In many ways he was the architect of the IAF's air superiority concept of June 1967. (AC)

of battle for a textbook relative-strength offensive, the IAF introduced fast turnarounds in order to tip the numerical scales in its favor.

This campaign concept was tested during Exercise *Lance*, from July 21 to 23, 1959. The exercise encompassed eight fighter squadrons with 121 aircraft and 110 pilots. Turnaround speed was emphasized as the key objective to allow a smaller force to perform more missions per day than a larger force. Total output of the eight squadrons was 1,020 sorties, an average of 42 sorties per squadron per day. Two-thirds of the pilots flew three to five missions per day. Turnaround timeframes were monitored in the two spearhead squadrons – Squadron 105 (Super Mystère) and Squadron 110 (Vautour) – and the average was 130 minutes.

15

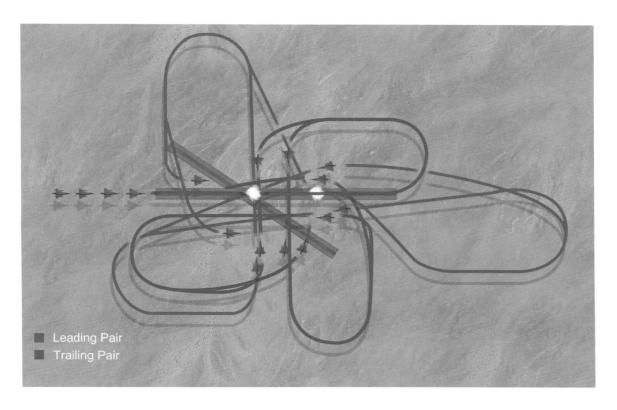

Leading Pair
Trailing Pair

ABOVE: STRAFING: THE 270 STRIKE PATTERN

The IAF did not dictate strike pattern. Bases, wings, and squadrons mostly preferred and practiced one of the three possible patterns. All three patterns were initiated with a bombing run along the axis of the targeted runway. The two pairs flew in trail about 2,000m apart. The pop-up maneuver took Mirages up to 6,000ft above ground level (AGL), and slower aircraft climbed to a slightly lower altitude in order to minimize exposure time to antiaircraft fire. The leading pair dived to bomb the farthest aiming point along the runway, while the trailing pair dived to bomb the nearest aiming point along the runway. The strikers exited the dive-bombing at an altitude of 1,000ft and were then to fly three strafing passes. It was then that the three strike patterns differed.

In the 270 strike pattern, the leading pair flew onwards for 15 seconds at 550 knots, turned left 270 degrees, lined abreast with each pilot picking a target and firing a one-second burst – roughly 20 rounds per gun – from 850 to 550m. The trailing pair flew past the farthest edge of the attacked runway, turned right 45 degrees, turned left 45 degrees, and then turned left 270 degrees to initiate the first strafing pass at a time when the first pair was turning towards the second strafing pass, and so on repeatedly with a phase of time and direction.

Five ranges were utilized, including three – Khalutsa, Matred, and Ovda – that simulated enemy air bases complete with runways, facilities, and aircraft. Range teams surveyed the targets after every raid. The two Mystère squadrons averaged a 17 percent gunnery score, having fired 8,513 rounds of which 1,437 hit the targets. A one-second burst from the Mystère's two guns expended some 40 rounds. During *Lance*, the two Mystère squadrons engaged up to about 200 targets and were expected to hit every target with at least six rounds, more than enough punch for the destruction of a parked aircraft.

Exercise *Sting*, from July 26 to 27, 1960, honed the IAF's air superiority skills. The six participating squadrons flew five missions per pilot per day, bombed runways, napalmed shelters, rocketed pens, and strafed aircraft. The IAF concluded that bombing accuracy assured suppression of runways until the arrival of the follow-up strike wave; the timeframe of a

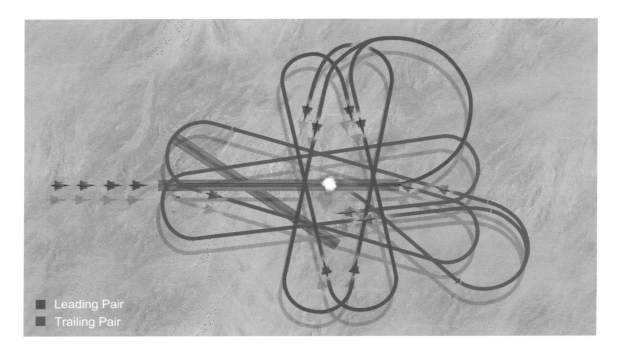

ABOVE: STRAFING: THE 180 TURN BACK STRIKE PATTERN

After the bombing run, the leading pair turned left 270 degrees for the first strafing pass and then two 180-degree turns for the second and third strafing passes. After the bombing run, the trailing pair turned right 45 degrees and then turned 180 degrees for the first strafing pass, followed by two more 180-degree turns for the second and third strafing passes. The 180 Turn Back strike pattern minimized time over target but narrowed the approach segments of the attackers, therefore potentially easing up on the defending antiaircraft gunners.

turnaround had been cut shorter in comparison with *Lance*, but for planning purposes was defined as two hours. Gunnery also yielded exceptional results. Out of 61 aircraft targets at Matred, 39 had been destroyed and 17 had been damaged. At Ovda, all 50 aircraft targets had been destroyed. The IAF was obviously aware that in the real world, targets would fire back, but even with some compensation for the worst, the *Sting* statistics were impressive and promising.

Six years prior to the Six-Day War, the IAF was fully ready to implement an air superiority campaign. The concept of small formations combining suppression and destruction, with fast turnaround to continue the offensive and accomplish objectives, had been forged. The following years would witness the IAF improving every conceivable aspect of the air superiority concept to the point of perfection at the right moment.

The IAF's order-of-battle aspirations were therefore derived from this air superiority campaign planning. Lessons from exercises indicated that a ratio of one fighter pilot per combat aircraft was insufficient. By April 1, 1962, the IAF had 181 fighter pilots, while the order of battle included 32 Super Mystères, 23 Vautours, 43 Mystères, 18 Ouragans, 16 Meteors, and 38 armed Fouga trainers for a total of 170 combat aircraft in eight squadrons. Seven days later, the IAF's strength was boosted when the first two Mirages were accepted. Within three years, its inventory had improved to 267 combat aircraft and armed trainers – 67 Mirages, 29 Super Mystères, 21 Vautours, 36 Mystères, 54 Ouragans, and 60 Fougas – in nine squadrons.

Exercise *Power* tested the IAF's air superiority concept – by then codenamed *Focus* – with an improvement: a continuous high tempo of missions instead of waves. The nine fighter

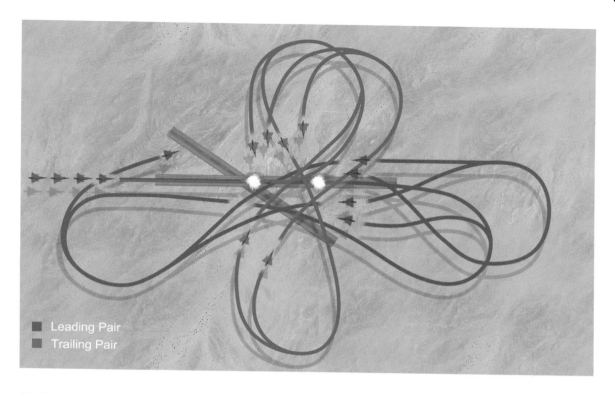

Leading Pair
Trailing Pair

ABOVE: STRAFING: THE 180 TURN INSIDE STRIKE PATTERN

The simplest and most straightforward of the three SEAB patterns. In the 180 Turn Inside pattern, after the bombing run, the leading pair turned left 270 degrees for the first strafing pass, then turned right 180 degrees for the second strafing pass, and then turned left 180 degrees for the third strafing pass. Meanwhile, the trailing pair – at the end of the bombing run – turned right 180 degrees for the first strafing pass, then turned left 180 degrees for the second strafing pass, and finally turned right 180 degrees again for the third strafing pass.

On top of the strengths and weaknesses of the 180 Turn Back pattern, the 180 Turn Inside pattern added even more simplicity but demanded much more coordination.

squadrons fielded 182 aircraft and 205 pilots, flew 1,031 sorties and averaged five sorties per pilot per day. Bombing accuracy averaged 77 percent and gunnery accuracy 16 percent.

Moti Hod succeeded Ezer Weizman as IAF Commander on April 27, 1966. Preparations for *Focus* continued, with Hod emphasizing simplicity. *Focus* planning had been growing in complexity, so the IAF command handover was timely and many observers later remarked that it was fortunate for the IAF that Weizman was in charge during preparations for *Focus* while Hod was in command during execution of *Focus*.

Aircraft

Around this time, the IAF sealed two major acquisition contracts for 48 A-4 Skyhawks and 50 Mirage 5s, with deliveries of both types scheduled to start in late 1967. Until that time, the IAF did not expect significant order of battle changes, except for the division of its Ouragan force into two squadrons, a move that was accomplished during the summer of 1966 as more fighter pilots became available. This set the IAF order of battle at nine fighter squadrons – three Mirages, two Mystères, two Ouragans, one Super Mystère, and one Vautour – plus a squadron of Fouga armed jet trainers.

OPPOSITE: AIR BASES OF ISRAEL, AND STRENGTHS, JUNE 5, 1967

Clashes along Israel's borders with Egypt, Jordan, and Syria intensified. Mirage pilots were credited with five air-to-air kills between July and November 1966: two Egyptian MiG-19s, two Syrian MiG-21s, and one Jordanian Hawker Hunter. Still, Israel did not expect a war in 1967.

The IDF plan for 1967 was presented in an IDF General Staff meeting on February 27, 1967. The IDF Intelligence Chief indicated that Arab solidarity was in a shambles and that Egypt was not intent on war. The IDF's concept was that the two principal indicators for a potential war were Egyptian military preparedness and Arab political solidarity. Egyptian military preparedness was considered insufficient, given the IDF's strength on one hand and Egypt's military involvement in Yemen on the other. Arab political solidarity was also considered too weak to support a war against Israel.

Nevertheless, the IDF prepared contingency plans for war. These emphasized the importance of air superiority for three reasons:

Israeli Prime Minister and Defense Minister Levy Eshkol – first from right – attending an IDF General Staff meeting on February 27, 1967, with IDF Chief of Staff Isaac Rabin to his right, IDF G Branch Chief Ezer Weizman fourth from left, IAF Commander Moti Hod third from left, and Command North Chief David Elazar second from left. (AC)

- The main IDF force consisted of reserve units, and enemy air strikes were viewed as a major threat to the swift mobilization of these reserves.
- Egypt's bomber force – some 60 Il-28s and Tu-16s – was viewed as a major threat to Israeli cities; in November 1963, the IDF had evaluated that Egypt's ability to attack Israel in a single bombing wave was 330 tons of bombs, and that by 1965 this potential would increase to 1,400 tons of bombs per 24 hours. On October 1, 1966, IDF Intelligence evaluated the potential at 315 tons per wave, based upon a serviceability of 65 percent, which corresponded with a maximum potential of 485 tons per wave.

SYRIA

GOLAN
HEIGHTS

Mediterranean Sea

1 Wing Ramat David

Megiddo

WEST
BANK

Base 15 Dov Field

Tel Aviv

Base 27 Lod

Base 8 Ekron

Jerusalem

4 Wing Khatsor

GAZA

Teman Field

6 Wing Khatserim

ISRAEL

SINAI

JORDAN

EGYPT

Eilat

N

| 0 | | | 40 miles |
| 0 | | 40km | |

---

1 WING RAMAT DAVID:

Squadron 109, Mystere inventory 16; serviceable 15, including 8 deployed to Ekron.

Squadron 110, Vautour inventory 19; serviceable 18 including 8 deployed to Ekron.

Squadron 117, Mirage inventory 24; serviceable 24.

BASE 15 DOV FIELD

Squadron 100, inventory 69, mostly Pipers; serviceable 62 including deployments to Megiddo and Teman Field as well as aircraft assigned to bases and wings.

Squadron 145, Herald inventory 5; serviceable 5.

BASE 27 LOD

Squadron 107, Ouragan inventory 16; serviceable 15.

Squadron 120, Dakota inventory 16; serviceable 14 including deployment to Sirkin.

Squadron 120, Stratocruiser inventory 7; serviceable 5.

BASE 8 EKRON

Squadron 103, Nord inventory 23; serviceable 20 including deployment to Sirkin.

Squadron 114, Super Frelon inventory 4; serviceable 4.

Squadron 116, Mystere inventory 17; serviceable 17.

Squadron 119, Mirage inventory 19; serviceable 19.

Squadron 123, Bell 47 inventory 13; serviceable 12 including helicopters deployed to Command South divisions.

Squadron 124, Sikorsky 58 inventory 28; serviceable 28.

Plus eight Squadron 109 Mysteres and eight Squadron 110 Vautours deployed from Ramat David.

4 WING KHATSOR

Squadron 101, Mirage inventory 22; serviceable 21.

Squadron 105, Super Mystere inventory 35; serviceable 35.

Squadron 113, Ouragan inventory 35; serviceable 33.

6 WING KHATSERIM

Squadron 147, armed Fouga inventory 44; serviceable 44.

TEMAN FIELD

Squadron 100, Flight C.

EILAT

Runway Unit 666.

MEGIDDO

Squadron 100, Flight B.

- IAF support to the IDF in an environment of air superiority was viewed as vital for Israel's defense doctrine: fighting on enemy soil a short war with unambiguous outcome.

It was then, on March 16, 1967, that IAF AIR3 issued Operation Plan 67/11 Operation *Focus*. The objective of *Focus* was the accomplishment of air superiority through the destruction of the EAF, as well as other Arab air forces as needed. The contingency plan covered four eventualities:

- *Focus A* against Egypt.
- *Focus B* against Syria.
- *Focus C* against Egypt and Syria, or against Egypt, Syria, and Jordan.
- *Focus D* against Egypt, Syria, Jordan, Lebanon, and Iraq.

The four *Focus* eventualities differed primarily in the task assignment program of the first wave; all other building blocks of the plan were similar. The concept's cornerstone was four-ship formations attacking enemy air bases at 15-minute intervals, with bombing to suppress runways and strafing to destroy aircraft.

Targets in Egypt were divided into four groups:

- Sinai air bases: Bir Gafgafa, Bir Tamada, El Arish, and Jabel Libni.
- Suez Canal air bases: Abu Sueir, Fayid, and Kabrit.
- Cairo and River Nile Delta air bases: Cairo West and Inchas.
- Upper Egypt air bases: Beni Suef, Luxor, Minya, and Ras Banas.

The less-capable combat aircraft, Ouragans and Mystères, were tasked to attack air bases in Sinai and the Suez Canal area. Super Mystères were tasked to raid air bases up to the Nile Delta, while Mirages and Vautours were tasked to strike air bases up to Upper Egypt.

A Squadron 116 Mystère and Squadron 119 Mirage inside a HAS at Ekron in March 1967. Having planned to win any air war by striking airfields, the IAF was aware that the enemy could do the same. But since HAS were costly, the IAF built only enough to protect a certain percentage of the inventory, given that some aircraft were always being serviced. (ARC)

Weapons

Over the enemy airfields, destruction would be meted out by bombs and guns. Only the Ouragans were armed with T-10 rockets in addition to bombs and guns. Every bomb was equipped with two detonators, one in the nose and one in the tail. The standard fit was the impact detonator in the nose and a 7–15-second delay detonator in the tail. Pilots had to select the delay detonator when attacking runways so that the bomb would explode after penetrating the surface, creating a deeper and larger crater that would take longer to repair. If a pilot wanted to bomb a target other than a runway – i.e. parked aircraft – then the nose impact detonator would be selected. Formations tasked to bomb concrete runways had the nose impact detonator replaced by a 0.1-second short delay detonator. At the time of the issue of Operations Order 67/11, the IAF possessed a small stock of light runway-piercing bombs and only Mystères and Super Mystères had been qualified to utilize the light runway-piercing bombs, so in the original *Focus A* task assignment program only six out of 38 formations were tasked to strike with light runway-piercing bombs.

The strike pattern was a single bombing run along the runway axis. Only the Ouragans were authorized to fly two runs against runways, with bombing in the first run and rocketry in the second; only the Vautours armed with eight 70kg bombs could fly two bombing runs, dropping four bombs in each run. Up to four strafing passes were then to be flown. The decision on how many strafing passes to fly – considering antiaircraft fire and fuel state – was delegated to formation leaders, with a single constraint: to clear the target area prior to the time-over-target of the follow-up formation.

Formations would fly to the targets, at least initially, at low altitude to avoid radar detection and then pop up to the minimum altitude that would allow a 35-degree dive-bombing attack. The aircraft would then glue to the deck and return for strafing, during which the guideline was to fly no higher than 1,500ft above ground level in order to minimize the efficiency of radar-guided antiaircraft artillery (AAA). Disengagement would be at low altitude until out of the areas defended by SA-2 missiles, whereupon a climb to economic cruise altitude and a flight straight back to base were the AIR3 recommendations.

Five days after Nasser ordered his army to march into Sinai, the first of Israel's Mirage 5 strike aircraft first flew in France. Three days earlier, four IAF pilots had traveled to the USA for an A-4 Skyhawk conversion course. The 48 A-4 Skyhawks and 50 Mirage 5s were scheduled to enter the IAF from autumn 1967, perhaps adding a motivation for Nasser to initiate the crisis in the summer. (BIAF)

The plans

The whole of the IAF's combat aircraft inventory was to be committed to the *Focus* first wave, except for 12 Mirages tasked to maintain quick reaction alert; each of the three Mirage squadrons fielding one pair on immediate readiness and a second pair to take over immediate alert if the first pair was scrambled.

Right from the start of *Focus*, the Fouga armed trainers squadron would be available to support the IDF, as would IAF transports, helicopters, and light spotting aircraft. Mirage and Vautour reconnaissance aircraft would photograph the enemy air bases towards the end of the first wave, while AIR4 would collect reports from formation leaders, at first over the radio while airborne after the attack, and then a fuller post-landing debrief via secured communication lines from bases to headquarters. AIR4 would then analyze the data and deliver the analyzed data to AIR3 for planning of the second wave. If no new Mission Order had been issued to a formation leader returning from a first-wave mission, then the *Focus* guideline was to repeat the first-wave mission during the second wave, and so on until the end of the day.

The original *Focus A* task assignment program included 38 formations tasked to attack enemy air bases with a total of only 154 aircraft. This was a conservative initial planning, well below the maximum IAF order of battle, in order to allow for aircraft to be grounded for reasons of normal serviceability and deep maintenance; the IAF Mission Order system at that time was squadron/counter, with the counter zeroed at midnight so that Mission Order 107/1 was the first mission order that AIR3 issued to Squadron 107 on a certain date:

Focus A task assignment program March 16, 1967							
Target	H-Hour	H+5	H+15	H+20	H+30	H+45	H+90
El Arish	107/1[1]	–	107/2[1]	–	–	107/3[1]	–
Jabel Libni	109/1[2]	–	109/2[3]	–	–	109/4[2]	–
Bir Gafgafa	113/1[1]	–	109/3[3]	–	–	113/3[1]	–
Bir Tamada	116/1[2]	–	116/3[3]	–	–	113/4[1]	–
Kabrit	119/5[6]	–	117/2[6]	–	–	116/4[3]	113/6[1]
Fayid	116/2[2]	–	113/2[1]	–	–	113/5[1]	113/7[1]
Abu Sueir	117/1[6]	–	105/2[8]	–	–	117/3[6]	117/4[6]
Inchas	–	105/1[7]	–	105/3[7]	–	105/4[7]	105/5[8]
Cairo West	–	101/1[6]	–	119/6[6]	101/2[6]	101/3[6]	–
Beni Suef	–	–	–	–	101/4[6]	119/7[6]	–
Minya	–	–	–	–	110/1[4]	110/2[5]	–
Luxor	–	–	–	–	110/3[4]	110/4[5]	–

Notes:
1 Four Ouragans with two 250kg bombs and eight T-10 rockets per aircraft
2 Four Mystères with two 250kg bombs per aircraft
3 Four Mystères with six light runway-piercing bombs per aircraft
4 Four Vautours with eight 70kg bombs per aircraft
5 Five Vautours with eight 70kg bombs per aircraft
6 Four Mirages with two 500kg bombs per aircraft
7 Four Super Mystères with two 250kg bombs per aircraft
8 Four Super Mystères with six light runway-piercing bombs per aircraft

AIR3 stressed three scenarios for activation of *Focus*:
- 72 hours' notice for *Focus* combined with a parallel IDF ground offensive.
- 24 hours' notice for *Focus* as a stand-alone operation without a parallel IDF offensive.
- Immediate activation of *Focus* to counter an enemy surprise strike.

The *Focus* activation order would be 'Activate *Focus* D-Day H-Hour', with follow-up orders concerning readiness level, reserves' mobilization, units' deployments, and updates of the *Focus* task assignment program. Squadrons were to prepare detailed briefings and maps for each *Focus* Mission Order, while all pilots – all pilots! – were ordered to learn their formation's mission, target, and enemy, as well as those of other squadrons.

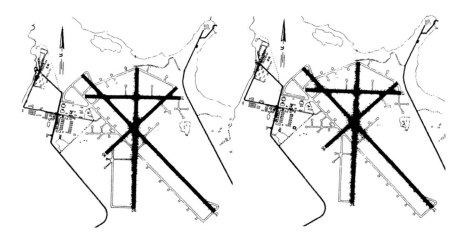

AIR4 circulated among IAF fighter pilots spot-the-difference games in order to encourage awareness of the SEAB mission; in this one there are ten differences between the two images of Kabrit. (AC)

DEFENDERS' CAPABILITIES
Nasser's Soviet air armada

The Suez campaign had given the EAF experience of being the target of an air superiority campaign. Beginning at H-Hour, 2015hrs on October 31, 1956, Anglo-French air forces raided Egyptian air bases with devastating impact. The Anglo-French air superiority concept required nighttime bombings to suppress runways and daytime strikes to destroy aircraft. The planners expected to achieve air superiority within 48 hours. Prior to H-Hour, the Anglo-French forces had flown 11 photographic reconnaissance sorties over Egypt to establish the EAF order of battle. Processed photographs revealed that the EAF's inventory at the start of the campaign included 110 MiG-15s, 48 Il-28s, 44 Vampires, and 14 Meteors. Obviously, aircraft parked or stored inside hangars could not have been detected through aerial photography, but such aircraft were likely to be unserviceable and therefore irrelevant to the actual order of battle. Similarly, Anglo-French forces flew post-strike reconnaissance missions in order to analyze the impact by counting destroyed aircraft. Royal Air Force battle damage assessment concluded that Anglo-French forces had destroyed on the ground 91 MiG-15s, 26 Il-28s, 30 Vampires, and 11 Meteors – 73 percent of the EAF order of battle at the start of the campaign. Given that a unit is usually defined as 'destroyed' with more than 50 percent losses, the EAF was virtually wiped out and the Anglo-French forces accomplished air superiority.

Ten years later, the EAF fielded more aircraft, but their air base infrastructure was generally similar to 1956, with intersecting runways and no hardened shelters for aircraft. Over the same timeframe, the IAF had completed the hardening of its air bases to provide a hardened aircraft shelter for most combat aircraft. However, although the IAF's construction of hardened aircraft shelters was sufficient for normal aircraft serviceability percentages, over the three weeks of crisis that preceded the war, serviceability increased to almost 100 percent; there were more serviceable combat aircraft than available hardened aircraft shelters. The EAF, on the other hand, does not seem to have improved serviceability during the period of the crisis, and in any case had no hardened aircraft shelters. Its only available shelters

French battle damage assessment images of Luxor from November 4, 1956, with interpreters pinpointing 17 destroyed Il-28s marked in circles, some still smoking, plus one – in a rectangle – seemingly intact. Still, the EAF did not attempt to harden bases in the wake of the 1956 war, and by 1967 there were still no HAS in Egypt. (AC)

OPPOSITE: AIR BASES OF EGYPT, SYRIA, JORDAN, IRAQ AND LEBANON, AND STRENGTHS, JUNE 5, 1967

were open pens with concrete walls that had been built in the bomber bases and in the forward fields.

IAF AIR4 evaluation of EAF deployment of combat aircraft in April 1965[1]			
Base	Squadron	Type	Notes
El Arish	18	MiG-17	Small squadron with an inventory of ten to 12 aircraft and a cadre of ten to 12 pilots.
Jabel Libni	–	–	Empty except for six retired MiG-15s positioned as dummies.
Bir Gafgafa	–	–	Empty owing to runway renovation work.
Kabrit	16 and 25	MiG-17	
Kabrit	24 and 31	MiG-15/17	Conversion units.
Fayid	20 and 27	MiG-19	
Abu Sueir	40	MiG-21	New squadron activated in March 1965.
Abu Sueir	73, 85, and 92	Il-28	Plus Flight 74 for maritime strike; about a dozen aircraft deployed to Yemen.
Inchas	17	MiG-17	Inactive.
Inchas	19 and 45	MiG-21	
Cairo West	–	MiG-21	Conversion unit.
Cairo West	88	Tu-16	Including a two-aircraft deployment to Yemen since December 1964.

Notes:
1 At that time AIR4 evaluated that the EAF order of battle included 95 MiG-15/17s, 18 MiG-19s, 60 MiG-21s, 25 Il-28s, and 16 Tu-16s

EAF bases had not changed much since 1956. The most profound change had been substantial lengthening of some runways to enable operations by supersonic fighters and heavy bombers – but the EAF had many airfields and most of these were quite far from Israel. Complacently, the EAF seems to have believed that the smaller and shorter-legged IAF would not be able to conduct an air superiority campaign as the Anglo-French forces had done a decade before. The EAF deployment had merits and drawbacks for both sides. For the Israelis, the distance made a campaign against the bases more difficult, but for the Egyptians, having a large number of distant bases obviously posed command and control issues. Except for bombers, the EAF's combat aircraft also mostly lacked the range to operate effectively against Israel unless deployed to forward airfields.

Extensive assets defended Egypt in general, and EAF bases in particular, from air strikes. Radar stations controlled most of Egypt's airspace. SA-2 surface-to-air missile batteries' overlapping arcs of engagement covered the whole of Egypt's heartland, plus specific strategic sites such as the Aswan Dam. Egypt also fielded hundreds of AAA weapons. However, the radar stations were unable to detect aircraft flying at very low level and the SA-2 batteries could not engage aircraft flying at low level. The AAA was organized in two independent AAA divisions, while each armored division had six AAA battalions and each infantry division had five. Batteries from the two independent AAA divisions were deployed to defend EAF bases.

The IAF had been monitoring the EAF's training for years and concluded that, in the event of hostilities, the EAF would divide available units into the following order of battle:

Hama ✈

T-4 ✈

LEBANON

SYRIA

Beirut ✈ Rayaq ✈
Beirut ● Dumayr ✈
Damascus ● Saikal ✈
Mazzeh ✈

Baly ✈

GOLAN
HEIGHTS

Mafraq ✈

WEST
BANK

Tel Aviv ● Amman ✈
Amman ●

Jerusalem ●

GAZA

ISRAEL JORDAN

Mediterranean Sea

Dekheila ✈

Mansoura ✈
El Arish ✈
Abu Sueir ✈ Jabel Libni ✈
Bilbeis ✈
Inchas ✈ Bir Gafgfa ✈ SINAI
Cairo West ✈ Fayid ✈ Kabrit ✈ Bir Tamada ✈
Cairo ● Cairo International ✈
Almaza ✈
Helwan ✈

EGYPT

Beni Suef ✈

Minya ✈

Hurghada ✈

N

0 ———— 80 miles
0 ———— 80km

Luxor ✈ ✈ Ras Banas ↘

EGYPT
El Arish: 7 MiG-17s.
Jabel Libni: 2 MiG-15/17s.
Bir Gafgafa: 14 MiG-21
Bir Tamada: 14 MiG-17s.
Abu Sueir: 27 Il-28s, 19 MiG-21s.
Fayid: 14 MiG-19s, 14 MiG-21s,
14 Su-7s.
Kabrit: 29 MiG-15s, 22 MiG-17s.
Inchas: 32 MiG-21s.
Cairo West: 22 MiG-15/17s,
15 MiG-21s, 15 Tu-16s.
Beni Suef: 15 Tu-16s.
Hurghada: 14 MiG-19s, 8 MiG-21s.
Almaza: 55 Il-14s, 20 Mi-4s, 12 Mi-6s.
Cairo International: 25 An-12s.
Dekheila: 3 Il-14s, 5 Mi-4s.
Bilbeis: EGAF Academy flying school
base, AIR4 did not specify based aircraft
on the morning of 5 June 1967.
Mansura: AIR4 did not specify based
aircraft on the morning of 5 June 1967.
Helwan: Egypt aerospace industry
airfield, AIR4 did not specify based
aircraft on the morning of 5 June 1967.
Minya: AIR4 did not specify based
aircraft on the morning of 5 June 1967.
Luxor: AIR4 did not specify based
aircraft on the morning of 5 June 1967.
Ras Banas: AIR4 did not specify based
aircraft on the morning of 5 June 1967.

IRAQ (NOT SHOWN)
H-3: 12 Hunters.
Habbaniya: 36 Hunters, 10 Tu-16s.
Rashid: 32 MiG-21s, 23 airlifters
including 8 An-12s and 2 Tu-124s,
20 Wessexes, 8 Mi-4s.
Kirkuk: 11 Il-28s, 20 MiG-17s,
14 Mi-4s.
Mosul: 7 Mi-4s.
Shaibah: 10 MiG-15s, 20 Jet Provosts.

JORDAN
Amman: 5 C-47s, 2 Doves, 4 Alouettes.
Mafraq: 24 Hunters.

LEBANON
Beirut: 6 Vampires.
Lebanon/Rayaq: 13 Hunters,
12 Vampires, 5 Alouettes.

SYRIA
Baly: 12 MiG-17s.
Mazzeh: 20 MiG-17s, 2 Il-28s,
5 Il-15s, 10 Mi-4s.
Dumayr: 40 MiG-21s.
Saikal: 15 MiG-21s.
T-4: 5 MiG-21s.
Hama: 3 MiG-17s.

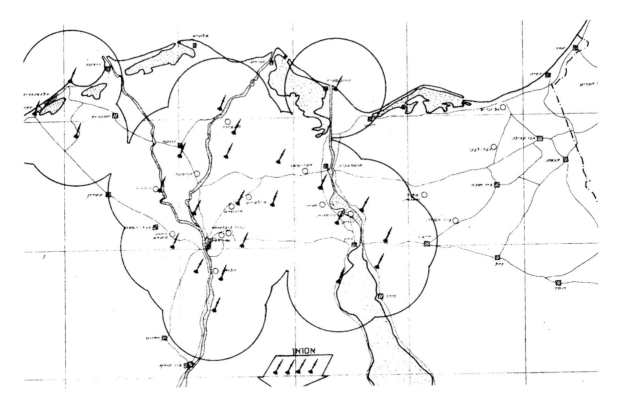

AIR4 evaluated that the Egyptian SA-2 engagement envelope covered the Nile Delta and the Suez Canal Zone, plus Alexandria's port and the Aswan dam; IAF formation leaders were advised to remain as low as possible during ingress as well as while attacking, and to climb to cruise only after leaving the envelope of the SA-2s. This was deemed protection enough, and the IAF did not plan preliminary strikes on radar stations or SA-2 batteries. (AC)

- For air defense and escort: six MiG-21 squadrons.
- To strike the IAF's airfields: half a squadron of Tu-16s, one and a half squadrons of Il-28s, two MiG-19 squadrons, and two MiG-15/17 squadrons.
- For air support: one flight of Il-28s and two MiG-15/17 squadrons.
- For bombing of cities and strategic targets: half a squadron of Tu-16s and one squadron of Il-28s.

During offensive operations, the fighters were expected to operate in large formations – not less than four and usually eight – while the bombers were expected to operate in cells of three, six, or nine aircraft.

For defense, MiG-21s would be on immediate alert, ready to scramble from six bases. The evaluated timeframes for dispatch of offensive operations – from order to departure – was two hours for fighters and three to four hours for bombers.

EAF Command East issued Operation Order 67/7 on May 27, 1967, as an amendment to Operation Order 67/2 from May 21. The objective was to raid IAF bases in order to achieve air superiority; this confirmed, after the event, IAF AIR4's evaluation of how the EAF would operate offensively: Squadron 18 was tasked to raid Ekron with 12 MiG-17s at H-Hour; Brigade 65 was tasked to bomb Khatsor at H-Hour with six Tu-16s.

CAMPAIGN OBJECTIVES
Securing air superiority

The *Focus* task assignment program was updated on April 10, 1967, in the wake of a major clash between Israel and Syria three days before. Yet, for a while, the IDF evaluation that Arab solidarity was too weak for war held on, and the volatile situation was expected to calm down. Then something happened. Amazingly – and almost without precedent in history – it is not clear what exactly happened. The most common explanation is that on May 13 the USSR fed its Arab allies with false information that Israel had amassed 13 brigades opposite the Israeli-Syrian border. The following day, the SAF flew a reconnaissance mission over northern Israel, slightly west of the Israeli-Syrian border. Whatever the outcome of the SAF reconnaissance mission, the next day Egypt initiated a massive and public deployment of forces to the Sinai Peninsula, opposite the Egyptian-Israeli border. Postwar, IAF Commander Moti Hod recalled:

> I received the message [of Egypt's deployment] on the stage in the stadium. It was one of the few Independence Days that I viewed from the ground. I usually flew [during Israel Independence Day's flyovers] but that year there was no flyover [of] Jerusalem, only a meager parade in line with the Armistice Agreements.
>
> The truth is that at first I did not take it seriously… Marching forces through Cairo looked like a psychological exercise and I accepted [the] IDF Intelligence evaluation – which at that time was shared by almost the whole of Israel – that for as long as Nasser was messed up with 90,000 soldiers in Yemen he would not decide to start a war so simply.

The deployment smashed the IDF's assessment that war was not expected in 1967. Still, the IDF evaluation that Egypt's armed forces were not up to the task was correct, and the American CIA issued similar evaluations during the crisis. Therefore, the puzzling figure in the crisis was Nasser, who had initiated the situation on May 14–15, escalated the crisis on May 23, and had failed to realize when the time was right to back off from the Israeli border and to lift the Red Sea maritime blockade.

IAF Commander Moti Hod presents a Mirage with a Syrian kill marking to Post Minister Israel Isaiah on May 10, 1967, at the ceremony that marked the issue of three stamps depicting IAF aircraft from the 1948 war (an Auster), the 1956 war (a Mystère), and from 1967 (a Mirage). Within a month, the Mirage would become the iconic jet of the 1967 war. (ILGP/PO and AC)

OPPOSITE: TYPICAL EAF BASE LAYOUTS

Abu Sueir and Bir Tamada were on the opposite ends of the scale of EAF bases. For IAF pilots, the concept of attacking Abu Sueir and Bir Tamada was similar: suppress runways (at aiming points 1, 2, 3), destroy aircraft, and ignore facilities. Abu Sueir was a large main air base that had been in existence for dozens of years, with extensive facilities that supported at least three resident squadrons of Il-28 bombers and MiG-21 interceptors (Il-28s at point 4; MiG-21s at 5). Bir Tamada was a small forward airfield that was nearly new – IDF Intelligence indicated only on October 1, 1966, that the airfield had been opened – but with rudimentary facilities that supported the deployment of a single MiG-17 squadron (resident MiG-17s at 4; the visiting Il-14 transports at 5, and Mi-4 and Mi-6 helicopters at 6, 7).

Bir Tamada was typical of the newer-concept airfields with a single runway. Obviously, all air bases positioned facilities around a runway or runways in order to enable operation of aircraft. Without aircraft, air bases are expensive, useless real estate; *Focus* therefore targeted aircraft. Bombing runways was not in order to destroy them but only to suppress them, to ease the destruction of aircraft. Facilities were initially ignored and were only strafed in subsequent strikes once pilots were unable to find intact aircraft. Once the destruction of aircraft had been completed – destruction of a military unit is usually defined as destruction of at least 50 percent of the unit's fighting assets – there was no point attacking the base further.

Egypt's blockade of the Straits of Tiran was an unambiguous *casus belli*, yet Israel was determined to exhaust diplomacy, a determination that at the time was wrongly presented as weakness. It was actually this seeming hesitation that enabled Israel to mobilize reserves easily, to hone the skills of the reserves in hasty training, and to exploit resources fully, up to almost 100 percent serviceability, a level of readiness and serviceability that was probably without precedent, that has possibly not been accomplished since, and which can be directly attributed to the crisis management skills of Egypt and Israel.

The IAF entered the crisis with 147 serviceable combat aircraft and the IDF fielded 954 serviceable tanks. By June 2, Israel concluded that diplomacy had been exhausted. The Israeli plan for war was offense against Egypt and defense against Jordan and Syria. The objective of the IAF was to destroy EAF aircraft in order to win air superiority, while the IDF's objective was to destroy the Egyptian armor in Sinai in order to eliminate the Egyptian threat to the existence of Israel and lift the Egyptian blockade of the Straits of Tiran. At the end of the slide to war, the IAF fielded 197 serviceable combat aircraft and the IDF had 1,093 serviceable tanks.

Orders of battle

Israel faced a coalition of at least four Arab nations: Egypt, Iraq, Jordan, and Syria. The IAF-presented nominal relative strength was 203 Israeli combat aircraft versus 602 Egyptian, Iraqi, Jordanian, Lebanese, and Syrian.

Base/Wing	Squadron	Type	Inventory	Serviceable	Pilots
1 Ramat David	109	Mystère	16	15	22 including 7 reservists
	110	Vautour	19	18	25 including 7 reservists
	117	Mirage	24	24	29 including 4 reservists
4 Khatsor	101	Mirage	22	21	28 including 3 reservists
	105	Super Mystère	35	35	37 including 10 reservists
	113	Ouragan	35	33	34 including 14 reservists
6 Khatserim	147	Fouga	44	44	42 including 29 reservists
8 Ekron	116	Mystère	17	17	22 including 5 reservists
	119	Mirage	19[2]	19	19[3]
27 Lod	107[4]	Ouragan	16	15	19 including 3 reservists

IAF fighter force order of battle, June 5, 1967[1]

ABU SUEIR

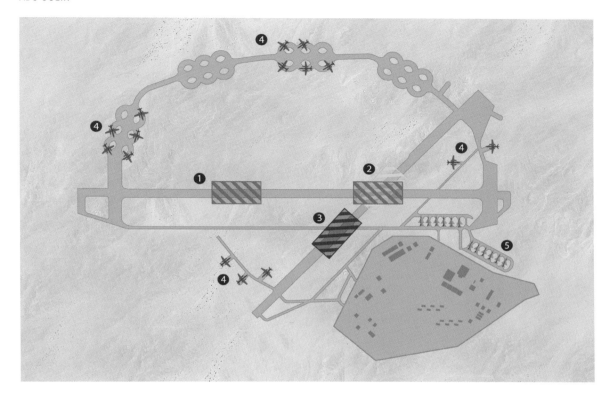

BIR TAMADA

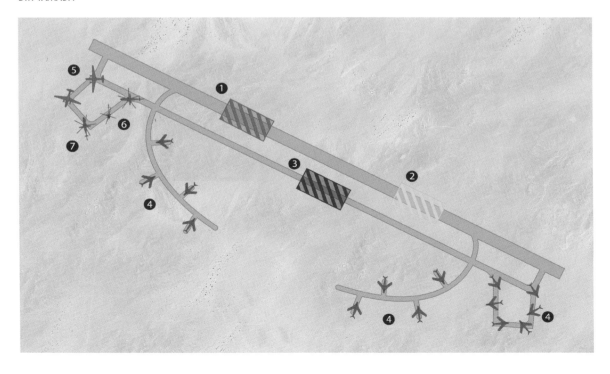

> **Notes:**
> 1 Total combat aircraft inventory 203, of which 197 were serviceable
> 2 Plus two reconnaissance Mirages
> 3 Only fighter force squadron without reservists
> 4 Deployed from Ramat David to Lod on 19 May 1967

However, Iraq was expected to deploy only a couple of squadrons to Jordan, while Lebanon was not officially allied with Egypt, Iraq, Jordan, and Syria. Actual IAF-presented nominal relative strength was therefore 203 Israeli combat aircraft versus 420 Egyptian, Jordanian, and Syrian combat aircraft. By June 5, the IAF had achieved 97 percent serviceability to field 197 combat aircraft that were expected to generate 985 sorties per 24 hours. If Arab serviceability was 66 percent, and if a serviceable Arab combat aircraft would have performed two to three sorties per 24 hours, then the combined capability of the EAF, the Jordanian Air Force (JAF), and the SAF would have been 560–840 sorties per 24 hours.

Israel's decision to launch a preemptive strike against Egypt further impacted the relative strength of the equation. Postwar, IAF Commander Moti Hod recalled:

I was certain that coordinated conduct of war between Egypt and Syria was impossible. As IAF Commander I had an edge, over other IDF commanders, in monitoring the aerial intelligence much more than they did [because] they were fed by [IDF] Intelligence without… an intimate knowledge of the other side. As IAF Commander it started with this small thing that I had an intimate knowledge of how they were flying every day… and I could know from where these four-ship formations departed and sometimes I could even know who the leaders of these four-ship formations were and over the years the relationship with the other side became almost personal… As a result, I firmly believed… that these two air forces, the Egyptian and the Syrian, were unable to react in coordination. To attack in coordination, yes [they could].

I knew that if I initiate [an attack] then the only option for Syrian conduct of war is to react. I knew that they were not ready for immediate reaction. I knew that they had a plan [for reaction] but in order to activate this plan they needed time. First of all they had to know that I started to attack [Egypt] and I knew that in Egypt it would take an hour to grasp what was happening… and then another hour to inform Syria… For this reason, the evaluation was that we would not face two aerial wars [at the same time]…

I have been accused that I accepted an uncalculated risk of committing all IAF [combat] aircraft to attack [the EAF] except for 12 Mirages for defense… but this was not the risk. The greatest risk was that we ignored an air force with 120 or 130 combat aircraft[2]… and offered it an opportunity to take an initiative… That was the greatest risk that [the] IAF took.

2   IAF AIR4 evaluated that the SAF fielded 97 combat aircraft, so perhaps Hod referred to the combined force of the SAF and JAF that IAF AIR4 evaluated at 121 combat aircraft.

Arab caricatures from the Waiting Period serve well to illustrate the atmosphere in the Middle East at the time. The four tanks surrounding Israel represented Egypt, Syria, Jordan, and Lebanon, while the eight Arab cannon barrels – representing Egypt, Syria, Jordan, Lebanon, Iraq, Saudi Arabia, Algeria, and Sudan – aim to push Israel back to the Mediterranean and into oblivion. These were both published in Lebanese newspapers on May 31, 1967. (ILGD/A)

The IAF-presented nominal relative strength between Egypt and Israel was 203 Israeli combat aircraft versus 299 Egyptian combat aircraft.

IAF AIR4 evaluation of Egyptian, Iraqi, Jordanian, Lebanese, and Syrian combat aircraft inventory, June 5, 1967						
	Egypt	Iraq	Jordan	Lebanon	Syria	Total
MiG-15/17	96	30	–	–	35	161
MiG-19	28	–	–	–	–	28
MiG-21	102	32	–	–	60	194
Su-7	16	–	–	–	–	16
Il-28	27	11	–	–	2	40
Tu-16	30	10	–	–	–	40
Hunter	–	48	24	13	–	85
Total	299	131	24	13	97	564

Bearing in mind serviceability and turnaround, the actual relative strength between the EAF and IAF, on the morning of June 5, 1967, was nowhere near the nominal numbers.

This Iraqi MiG-21 defected to Israel in August 1966. After the EAF flew MiG-21s over Dimona on May 26, 1967, the IAF placed it at readiness at Khatsor – alongside the Mirage QRA complex – as the fast-climbing MiG-21 might be better able to intercept high-speed, high-altitude intruders. Obviously, after *Focus* began, scrambling the IAF MiG-21 was unthinkable except in a catastrophic situation. (AC)

THE CAMPAIGN
One day in June

As the IDF wanted to seize El Arish intact, the *Focus* strikes on the airfield were limited to destroying AAA and then aircraft. IDF Command South occupied it on the morning of June 6, IAF Super Frelons airlifted in a Runway Unit later that day, and the first IAF airlifter, a Nord, landed that evening. This photo was taken from an IAF Piper during the war; note the undamaged runways, the UNEF compound at the lower left, and farther left the area where the resident MiG-17s had been destroyed. (AC)

Israel's armed forces had been fully mobilized since Egypt had blocked the Straits of Tiran on May 23, 1967. Egypt's armed forces were mostly regular and theoretically could have been fully deployed to Sinai indefinitely. Israel's armed forces were mostly reserves, and mobilization practically stalled regular life in Israel. Although the United States seemed unwilling to enforce its own 1957 guarantee of Israel's freedom of navigation through the Straits of Tiran, in clandestine talks it also seemingly gave Israel a green light to attack Egypt.

By June 2, the crisis had entered its 19th day, and the 11th day since Israel had initiated full mobilization. Regardless of all pre-crisis intelligence evaluations that Egypt was not yet ready to challenge Israel – evaluations that were correct – Nasser seemed determined to adhere to the course of confrontation, therefore leaving Israel no other option but to preempt.

The IDF had been refining plans, improving serviceability, and refreshing reserves up to a peak point that had been reached around June 2. That day, the IDF Chief presented to the Israeli government the then relative strength between the EAF and IAF, which was 213 EAF combat aircraft (including 156 fighters and 55 bombers[3]) versus 192 IAF fighter aircraft. Israel could hardly hope for a better relative-strength situation, and the Defense Minister recommended a preemptive offensive on June 5.

Focus had been activated in an IDF General Staff meeting that opened at 1900hrs on June 4, with D-Day June 5 and H-Hour 0745hrs. H-Hour selection had been based upon five principal parameters:

3   Presumably, presented numbers included only serviceable EAF combat aircraft in order to present a favorable relative strength that would encourage the ministers to approve an IDF preemptive offensive; and yes, the numbers as presented did not add up!

- The earliest practical H-Hour in order to enable the IAF to fly the maximum number of missions during Day 1: up to around 800 sorties at five sorties per aircraft per day, with allowance for attrition and serviceability; attrition was expected to mount along the timeline of *Focus*, while serviceability was expected to decline along the same timeline, mostly owing to aircraft returning from missions with some sort of battle damage that would affect turnaround times.
- IAF fighter pilots were expected to fly four to five missions per day, so the maximum possible sleeping time prior to H-Hour – minus two or three hours from wake-up to takeoff – was essential for physical fitness.
- Morning mists were a well-known phenomenon that could have hampered navigation, location, and aiming, especially for the first formations, which were crucial to ensure surprise and success; it was most important that all of the first nine formations would strike so that none of the enemy air bases would be able to react unhindered.
- The complicated radio silence taxi and takeoff drill had to be performed during daylight.
- H-hour was not to be an obvious one such as dawn or a full hour such as 0800hrs.

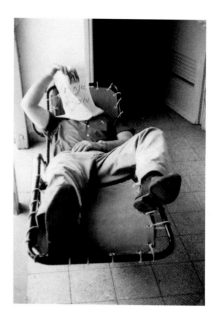

IAF Squadron 117 Mirage reserve pilot Dror Avneri was photographed during the Waiting Period, resting in the veranda of Squadron 117 headquarters, shading his face with a sheet of paper on which was written in Hebrew "WE ARE READY." (AC)

After the IDF General Staff meeting had been concluded, the IAF Commander convened base, wing, and squadron commanders for the final *Focus* orders group. AIR3 presented the updated *Focus* task assignment program. The final *Focus A* task assignment program included 45 formations – up from 38 on March 16 – tasked to attack enemy air bases with a total of 176 aircraft – up from 154 on March 16 – thus indicating the substantial improvement in IAF serviceability and readiness during the "Waiting Period" that preceded the Six-Day War. The final *Focus A* task assignment program had not been typed, in order to minimize exposure and maximize security:

The Squadron 101's briefing room's board on the morning of June 5, 1967, with the squadron's task assignment program and H-Hour 0745hrs added underneath. Pilots were to depart from the squadron's headquarters to the aircraft from 0650 to 0730hrs, to start engines from 0705 to 0745hrs, and to depart from 0717 to 0800hrs. (AC)

Focus A task assignment program, June 4, 1967										
	AIR4 evaluation of aircraft present	0745	0750	0755	0800	0810	0825	0840	0855	0910
El Arish	7 MiG-17s	107/1[1]	–	107/2[1]	–	–	–	–	–	–
Jabel Libni	2 MiG-15/17s[2]	–	–	–	–	–	–	–	–	–
Bir Gafgafa	14 MiG-21s	113/1[3]	–	113/8[3]	–	109/3[4]	113/3[3]	113/4[3]	–	–
Bir Tamada	14 MiG-17s	101/7[5]	107/4[3]	–	109/4[6]	113/6[3]	107/3[7]	–	–	–
Kabrit	29 MiG-15s and 22 MiG-17s	105/6[8]	–	105/8[8]	–	105/9[9]	109/1[6]	109/2[4]	–	–
Fayid	14 MiG-19s, 14 MiG-21s and 16 Su-7s	116/1[6]	–	113/2[3]	–	116/3[4]	113/5[3]	116/2[6]	–	113/7[10]
Abu Sueir	27 Il-28s and 19 MiG-21s	117/3[11]	–	117/5[12]	–	105/2[13]	110/4[14]	116/4[4]	105/7[8]	117/6[12]
Inchas	32 MiG-21s	–	119/5[12]	–	105/1[8]	105/4[13]	105/5[8]	105/3[8]	–	–
Cairo West	22 MiG-15/17s, 15 MiG-21s and 15 Tu-16s	–	101/3[12]	–	119/6[12]	101/4[15]	101/5[16]	117/4[12]	119/7[12]	–
Beni Suef	15 Tu-16s	–	–	–	–	110/1[14]	110/2[14]	101/6[12]	110/3[17]	–

Notes:
1 Four Ouragans with eight T-10 rockets per aircraft tasked to strike AAA emplacements and then strafe aircraft without bombing runways, since by then the IDF had been expected to occupy El Arish within 36 hours from H-Hour
2 Most likely retired airframes positioned as dummies, and since Jabel Libni had not been occupied by combat aircraft it had been removed from the list of Focus targets
3 Four Ouragans with two 250kg bombs and eight T-10 rockets per aircraft
4 Four Mystères with six light runway-piercing bombs per aircraft
5 Three Mirages with two 500kg bombs per aircraft tasked to bomb and then fly an offensive combat air patrol
6 Four Mystères with two 250kg bombs per aircraft
7 Three Ouragans with two 250kg bombs and eight T-10 rockets per aircraft
8 Four Super Mystères with two 250kg bombs per aircraft
9 Three Super Mystères with two 250kg bombs per aircraft
10 Five Ouragans with two 250kg bombs and eight T-10 rockets per aircraft
11 Four Mirages with two 500kg bombs per aircraft tasked to bomb and then fly an offensive combat air patrol
12 Four Mirages with two 500kg bombs per aircraft
13 Four Super Mystères with six light runway-piercing bombs per aircraft
14 Four Vautours with eight 70kg bombs per aircraft
15 Four Mirages with two 250kg bombs and two heavier runway-piercing bombs per aircraft
16 Three Mirages with two 500kg bombs per aircraft
17 Three Vautours with eight 70kg bombs per aircraft

The IAF Commander emphasized the importance of tactical surprise. The EAF may have been on readiness to face an IAF offensive, but the crucial elements of tactical surprise were timing and whereabouts. In order to accomplish tactical surprise, the IAF had to avoid detection of all flying formations up to H-Hour through flying very low with strict radio silence. The guidelines for pilots experiencing malfunctions were unambiguous:

- If a malfunction was encountered during departure, do whatever needed to make sure that the runway would remain serviceable for follow-up departures, even if this meant to veer away from the runway and crash beside it.

- If a malfunction was encountered while flying from base to target, do whatever needed – including ejection – except for climbing and transmitting (even though all IAF combat aircraft types except the Mirage were not equipped with zero-zero ejection seats and the low-altitude flight from base to target was well below the minimum altitude for safe ejection!)

Base, wing, and squadron commanders returned to the units at around 2100hrs, notified their deputies and hinted to the pilots through an order to go to sleep early and to get a good night's sleep in anticipation of a demanding day. Many pilots interpreted the hint correctly and could hardly sleep at all!

Sunrise was at 0438hrs and pilots were woken up around dawn. Commanders and deputies prepared briefing rooms, writing with white chalk on a blackboard the squadron's task assignment program and H-Hour, 0745hrs. Squadron briefings were concise, since the IAF had been preparing for *Focus* for weeks. Formation leaders then briefed the pilots under their command, and the pilots were transported to the dispersed aircraft – that had been configured and ready for *Focus* since May 23 – for preflight checks that were obviously more thorough than ever before. The complex taxi and departure drill in radio silence was then initiated, with traffic marshals positioned at key points with large signs that ordered pilots to stop or taxi.

Operation Order 67/11 *Focus* also included a number of support missions, and it was a *Focus* support mission that was the first aircraft to depart an IAF airfield on June 5: Squadron 120's Stratocruiser 97 departed Lod at 0325hrs with the AIR Department Chief – effectively the IAF's second-in-command – on board.

Focus support missions				
Squadron	Mission	Aircraft	Task	Details
101	101/1	2 Mirages	Air defense	Readiness for scramble as first pair from Khatsor.
101	101/2	2 Mirages	Air defense	Readiness for scramble as second pair from Khatsor.
103	103/1	1 Nord	Search and rescue	Readiness for scramble from Ekron.
110	110/5	1 Vautour IIB	Reconnaissance	Photograph EAF bases in Sinai at the end of *Focus* first wave.
110	110/6	2 Vautour IINs	Support	Jamming SA-2 off Port Said.
117	117/1	2 Mirages	Air defense	Readiness for scramble as first pair from Ramat David.
117	117/2	2 Mirages	Air defense	Readiness for scramble as second pair from Ramat David.
117	117/7	2 Mirages	Air defense	Escort Mission 110/6.
119	119/1	2 Mirages	Air defense	Readiness for scramble as first pair from Ekron.
119	119/2	2 Mirages	Air defense	Readiness for scramble as second pair from Ekron.
119	119/3	1 Mirage	Reconnaissance	Readiness from H+30 to photograph EAF bases.
119	119/4	1 Mirage	Reconnaissance	Photograph EAF bases Inchas, Abu Sueir, Fayid, and Kabrit at the end of *Focus* first wave.
120	120/3	1 Dakota	Intelligence	Listening/jamming.
120	120/4	1 Dakota	Radio relay	Takeoff at H-Hour.
120	120/5	1 Dakota	Radio relay	Takeoff at H-Hour.
124	124/1	1 S-58	Search and rescue	Readiness for scramble from Mitspe Ramon.
124	124/2	1 S-58	Search and rescue	Readiness for scramble from Khatserim.
124	124/3	1 S-58	Search and rescue	Readiness for scramble from Ekron.

At 0410hrs, a Piper departed Teman Field for a routine dawn patrol along the Egyptian-Israeli border, and at 0440hrs, another Piper departed Dov Field for a routine liaison flight.

At 0534hrs, a pair of Squadron 101 Mirages – radio callsign CLOSET[4] – scrambled from Khatsor for a seemingly routine morning patrol. At 0630hrs, a Piper departed Dov Field for a routine liaison flight, and from 0643 to 0650hrs, four Fouga trainers departed Khatserim with actual air cadets in the cockpits to fly training missions as though the IAF had been beginning a normal day. Two Pipers departed Teman Field at 0700hrs for routine liaison flights, thus concluding the IAF's impersonation of a normal day for the enemy's listening centers and radar stations.

First wave
Time Over Target 0745hrs

Six formations were tasked to strike at 0745hrs. The targets were three EAF forward fields in the Sinai Peninsula and three major EAF bases near the Suez Canal.

The four Ouragans of Mission 113/1 took off from Khatsor at 0714hrs tasked to attack targets 1 and 2 along Bir Gafgafa runway 15/33. SWEATHER reported that two bombs hit the runway. After their rocketry pass, a MiG-21 was spotted starting to take off. SWEATHER 3 strafed the rolling MiG-21, which caught fire, became airborne in flames, and crashed near the end of the runway. Another MiG-21 managed to take off from the cratered runway and SWEATHER 4 reported that this MiG-21 was last seen flying west. SWEATHER reported the destruction of five MiG-21s and hits on three helicopters. However, only SWEATHER 1 and 4 returned to Khatsor. The SWEATHER 2 pilot ejected over the Mediterranean Sea off the coast of the Gaza Strip and was taken prisoner; the IAF attributed the loss to antiaircraft fire. The crash site of SWEATHER 3 was pinpointed postwar, not far from Bir Gafgafa. Debris of rockets that the IAF identified as typical of Egyptian MiG-19s was found near the wreckage of the Ouragan. Postwar, IAF AIR1 attributed the loss of SWEATHER 3 to an EAF MiG-21 or MiG-19.

The four Mirages of Mission 117/3 departed Ramat David at 0715hrs to bomb targets 1 and 2 along Abu Sueir runway 09/27, and then headed east to patrol over Bir Gafgafa. At the same time, 0715hrs, Mission 116/1 departed Ekron tasked to bomb targets 1 and 2 along Fayid runway 09/27. MIKADO 3 aborted during ingress, so the three remaining aircraft of MIKADO flight dropped only six bombs.[5] MIKADO then ignored an An-12 transport that aborted its landing at Fayid after witnessing MIKADO's bombing. Prioritizing strafing of combat aircraft on the ground over an easy kill of an enemy transport in the air, MIKADO 1 reported destruction of between four and six MiG-21s and MIKADO 4 the destruction of two MiG-21s. MIKADO's total claim was 13 destroyed aircraft.

At Khatsor, the Super Mystères of Mission 105/6 left at 0719hrs to bomb targets 1 and 2

4   IAF radio callsigns at the time were in groups of a general callsign for a squadron, a specific callsign for formation leaders within a squadron, and numbers per pilots flying alone; for example, the Squadron 101 family name was FURNITURE, with specific callsigns for formation leaders such as CLOSET, SHELF, CURTAIN, COUNTER, DESKTOP, LAMP, SOFA, or CHANDELIER and specific numbers for pilots flying alone, such as 111 for Squadron Commander Amos Lapidot or 157 for Squadron 101 pilot Guri Palter, so that when they flew alone their identification radio callsign was FURNITURE 111 and FURNITURE 157 respectively.

5   However, Squadron 113's HAT reported – prior to its own attack – observing eight craters along runway 09/27. I note this to remind readers and researchers that all combat reports – though much more to be depended upon than memoirs and recollections – should always be taken with a pinch of salt.

along runway 13/31 of Kabrit air base. TOPAZ 2 and 3 returned to Khatsor separately and reported the destruction of eight to ten enemy aircraft on the ground at Kabrit – some of which may have been dummies – plus two Il-14s in the air. AIR4 scaled down the TOPAZ total to six aircraft destroyed. TOPAZ 2 reported that TOPAZ 1 and 4 hit the ground while turning at low altitude during an engagement with MiG-21s over northwest Sinai, but the possibility that the two Super Mystères had been shot down by enemy action cannot be ruled out. AIR1 Statistics at first credited the TOPAZ formation with two Il-14 kills, and AIR1 Statistics Amendment later credited TOPAZ 1 and 4 with one Il-14 kill each.

Mission 107/1 departed Lod at 0724hrs tasked to fire rockets at AAA emplacements within the El Arish airfield perimeter.[6] URTICA claimed the destruction of six MiGs as well as a damaged radar station within the perimeter of the airfield. A round hit URTICA 2 and a ricochet struck URTICA 3.

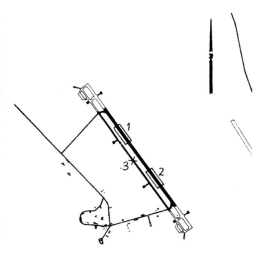

6   Original planning tasked the Ouragans to attack the El Arish runways, but since
      Focus was activated in parallel with an IDF offensive, and as Command South
      was expected to occupy El Arish, the tasking of the Ouragans was changed from
      bombing and rocketing runways prior to strafing aircraft to rocketing antiaircraft
      gun emplacements prior to strafing aircraft, so that the IAF would be able to operate
      from El Arish, in support of Command South, immediately after the conquest.

A simple IAF plan of Bir Gafgafa, the main EAF base in Sinai. Main bombing targets were marked with rectangles and secondary targets with "X." The IAF experimented with various bombing patterns and opted to bomb along the runway axis, with each pair of attacking aircraft aiming at a different point, to ensure the runway would become unserviceable after the bombing. (AC)

Squadron 101 Deputy A Dan Sever produced an exemplary debrief report in the wake of Mission 101/7 that he flew as SHELF 1. He is photographed here on June 9, occupying the seat of an Egyptian AAA gunner who may have fired at his Mirage on the morning of June 5. AIR4 evaluated that three AAA batteries defended Bir Tamada: two with four 57mm cannon each and one with six 14.5mm guns. The three batteries were deployed along the runway axis offset to the north. (AC)

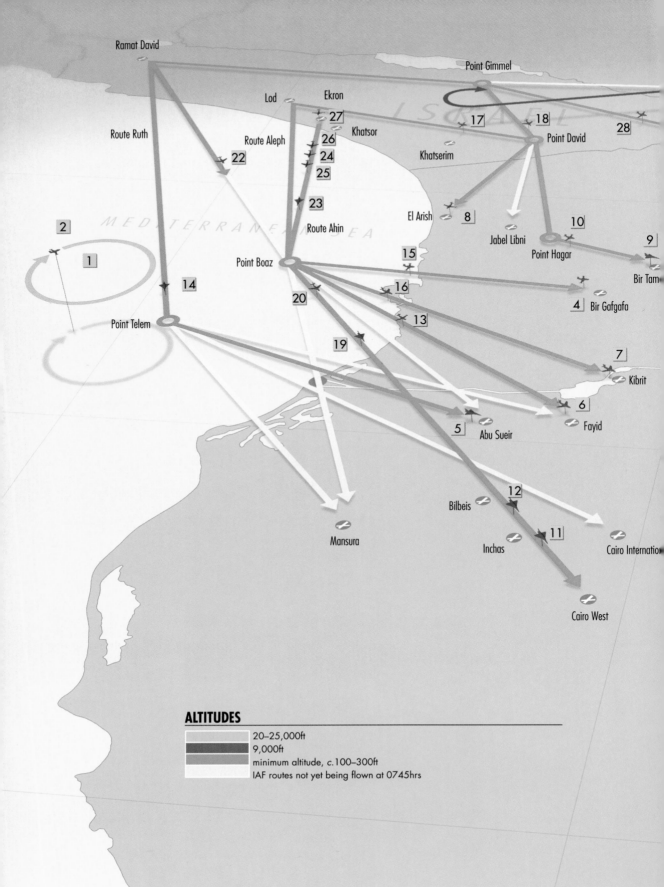

Ramat David

Point Gimmel

Lod   Ekron

Route Ruth   27
Route Aleph   Khatsor

22   26   Khatserim
24
25

23

Route Ahin   El Arish

ISRAEL   17   18   28
Point David

Khatserim

Jabel Libni   8   10   9
Point Hagar   Bir Tam

2   Point Boaz   15
1   16   4   Bir Gafgafa

14   20   13
Point Telem   7   Kibrit

19   6   Fayid
5   Abu Sueir

12
Bilbeis   11

Mansura   Inchas   Cairo International

Cairo West

MEDITERRANEAN SEA

ALTITUDES

20–25,000ft
9,000ft
minimum altitude, *c.*100–300ft
IAF routes not yet being flown at 0745hrs

3

| int
ch | ✈ 21 |

EVENTS

Support

1. Mission 110/6 Vautours were flying an EW mission to jam Egyptian SA-2 batteries

2. Mission 117/7, two escorting Mirages. Missions 110/6 and 117/7 both left Ramat David at 0721hrs

3. Mission 120/4, a C-47 radio relay mission over the Negev Desert

In addition, not shown:

Mission 120/3 was tasked to be over Ashkelon at H-Hour and to patrol between Ashkelon and Beer Sheva at 10,000ft

Mission 120/5 was to take off at H-Hour and to patrol west of Tel Aviv and north of El Arish, also for radio relay

ToT 0745hrs

4. The four Ouragans of Mission 113/1 SWEATHER took off from Khatsor at 0714hrs to attack targets 1 and 2 along Bir Gafgafa runway 15/33

5. The four Mirages of Mission 117/3 departed Ramat David at 0715hrs to bomb targets 1 and 2 along Abu Sueir runway 09/27

6. At the same time, 0715hrs, Mission 116/1 MIKADO Mystères departed Ekron to bomb targets 1 and 2 along Fayid runway 09/27.

7. At Khatsor, the Super Mystères of Mission 105/6 TOPAZ left at 0719hrs to bomb targets 1 and 2 along runway 13/31 of Kabrit air base.

8. Ouragans of Mission 107/1 URTICA departed Lod at 0724hrs to rocket AAA emplacements within the El Arish airfield perimeter

9. Mission 101/7 SHELF departed Khatsor at 0724hrs to bomb targets 1 and 2 along Bir Tamada runway 12/30.

ToT 0750hrs

10. Mission 107/4, callsign LILIUM, departed Lod at 0716hrs to attack targets 1 and 2 along Bir Tamada runway 18/30.

11. Mission 101/3, callsign CURTAIN, left Khatsor at 0717hrs to bomb targets 1 and 2 along Cairo West runway 16/34

12. Mission 119/5 APARTMENT departed Ekron at 0724hrs to bomb targets 1 and 2 along Inchas runway 04/22.

ToT 0755hrs

13. Mission 113/2, Ouragan, departed Khatsor at 0723hrs to bomb targets 1 and 2 along Fayid runway 09/27. Callsign HAT.

14. Mission 117/5 Mirage departed Ramat David at 0727hrs to bomb targets 1 and 2 along Abu Sueir runway 09/27.

15. At 0728hrs Mission 113/8 APRON departed Khatsor to bomb targets 1 and 2 along Bir Gafgafa runway 15/33.

16. Mission 105/8 LATIF Super Mystères departed Khatsor at 0730hrs to bomb targets 1 and 2 along Kabrit runway 13/31.

17. Just 20 minutes after the first formation took off, Mission 107/2 departed Lod at 0734hrs. It was tasked to rocket AAA emplacements as the second and final *Focus* formation to raid El Arish.

ToT 0800hrs

18. The Mystères of Mission 109/4, callsign COTTON, took off from Ramat David at 0723hrs to hit Bir Tamada runway 18/30 again.

19. Mission 119/6 LINTEL left Ekron at 0727hrs to bomb targets 1 and 3 on Cairo West runway 10/28.

20. Lastly in this wave, Mission 105/1 DUBEK departed Khatsor at 0733hrs to bomb targets 1 and 3 along Inchas runway 09/27.

ToT 0810hrs

21. TIGRIS, Mission 110/1, departed Ekron at 0717hrs, with eight 70kg bombs per Vautour, to strike targets 1 and 2 along Beni Suef runway 01/19.

22. CONCRETE, Mission 109/3, departed Ramat David at 0734hrs to strike Bir Gafgafa's runway 15/33.

23. Mission 101/4 departed Khatsor at 0737hrs to bomb targets 1 and 3 along Cairo West runway 10/28 with, probably, two 250kg bombs and two heavier runway-piercing bombs per Mirage.

24. Mission 116/3, GANDHI, departed Ekron at 0740hrs to strike targets 1 and 2 along Fayid runway 09/27 with six light runway-piercing bombs per Mystère.

25. Super Mystères of Mission 105/4 PRESIDENT departed Khatsor at 0740hrs to attack targets 1 and 2 along Inchas runway 04/22 with light runway-piercing bombs.

26. Mission 105/2 PERFECT departed Khatsor at 0742hrs to attack targets 1 and 2 on Abu Sueir runway 09/27 with light runway-piercing bombs

27. Ouragans of Mission 113/6 SHIRT departed Khatsor at 0745hr to attack targets 1 and 2 along Bir Tamada runway 12/30.

ToT 0825hrs

28. Mission 110/2 JORDAN departed Ramat David at 0725hrs to bomb targets 1 and 2 along Beni Suef runway 01/19. JORDAN started at low altitude, then exactly at H-Hour 0745hrs climbed towards the more efficient cruise altitude.

Mission 101/7 departed Khatsor at 0724hrs tasked to bomb targets 1 and 2 along Bir Tamada runway 12/30. Crosswinds hampered hits. SHELF 1 hit the southern edge of the runway with one bomb; its second bomb did not drop. The hits of SHELF 2 and 3 were not observed, but were probably misses owing to the crosswind. SHELF counted 11 MiG-17s, one An-12, two Mi-4s, and one Mi-6 on the ground at Bir Tamada, but did not strafe as it was tasked to patrol. While heading north to the patrol sector, SHELF saw an An-12 seemingly about to land at Bir Gafgafa. A MiG-21 was then observed flying at low altitude near Bir Gafgafa, so SHELF turned towards it, intending to return to the An-12 after shooting down the MiG. However, after the MiG-21 entered a spin and crashed, the An-12 had disappeared. SHELF completed an exemplary clear and concise debrief with a report that five aircraft were burning on the ground at Bir Gafgafa, thus confirming SWEATHER's claim. AIR1 Statistics did not credit a MiG-21 air-to-air kill to SHELF or to Squadron 101. AIR1 History attributed the MiG-21 loss to an accident. Eventually, SHELF 1 was credited with an air-to-air kill.

Time Over Target 0750hrs

The two formations that would attack Inchas and Cairo West had farther to fly over Egyptian territory to reach their targets. They were therefore timed to strike five minutes later, so that they would not cross the coastline too soon, and so avoid the remote possibility that an Egyptian observation post would spot the incoming aircraft and alert the EAF in time to scramble MiG-21s.

Also timed to strike at 0750hrs was the follow-up strike on Bir Tamada. The formation tasked to strike Bir Tamada – as well as that tasked to raid Abu Sueir from 0755hrs – followed a formation that bombed and then flew an offensive patrol over northwest Sinai, a twist that was added to the *Focus* plan during the Waiting Period as more and more aircraft became available.

Mission 107/4, callsign LILIUM, departed Lod at 0716hrs tasked to attack targets 1 and 2 along Bir Tamada runway 18/30. SHELF had probably failed to render the runway inoperable, so several MiG-17s managed to depart during the LILIUM attack. However, the departing MiG-17s did not engage the attacking Ouragans. LILIUM claimed destruction of eight MiG-17s (including two that were prepared to depart with pilots in the cockpits), two Il-14s, and three helicopters. LILIUM 3 claimed to have actually shot down a Mi-6 immediately after the big helicopter lifted from the ground, but this claim was not listed as an air-to-air kill in the postwar AIR1 Statistics.

Mission 101/3, callsign CURTAIN, left Khatsor at 0717hrs tasked to bomb targets 1 and 2 along Cairo West runway 16/34. AIR3 had assigned Squadron 101 to fly six four-ship missions in the *Focus* first wave, but Squadron 101 had only 21 serviceable Mirages so CURTAIN flew as a three-ship formation. Despite meticulous planning, the faster Mirages of CURTAIN overtook the slower Ouragans of SWEATHER during ingress – choosing to pass *below* the low-flying Ouragans, skimming the waves of the Mediterranean. CURTAIN reported that five bombs exploded on target. CURTAIN then flew three strafing passes and claimed the destruction of eight Tu-16s, three Il-28s, and three MiG-21s, while AIR4 later evaluated that CURTAIN had destroyed a total of ten aircraft.

Mission 119/5 departed Ekron at 0724hrs tasked to bomb targets 1 and 2 along Inchas runway 04/22. APARTMENT 1 claimed destruction of three MiGs, APARTMENT 2 claimed four MiGs, and APARTMENT 3 claimed two MiGs. APARTMENT 4 strafed six MiGs in three strafing passes, claiming the destruction of four for sure and two with doubt.

Time Over Target 0755hrs

Five IAF formations were tasked to strike, from 0755hrs, two EAF airfields in Sinai and the three EAF bases west of the Suez Canal. The IAF had already attacked eight EAF bases, and claimed the destruction of up to 79 aircraft on the ground plus four aircraft in the air, for the loss of just four aircraft. Mission 113/2 departed Khatsor at 0723hrs tasked to bomb targets 1 and 2 along Fayid runway 09/27. Callsign HAT, this was the first Ouragan formation to cross the Suez Canal during the Six-Day War. The Ouragans arrived two minutes earlier than planned and the MIKADO Mystères of Squadron 116 were still over Fayid. Burning aircraft generated a lot of smoke, that eased navigation but also obscured targets. HAT 3 crashed north of Fayid after the first strafing pass, possibly owing either to antiaircraft fire or to controlled flight into terrain. HAT reported a lot of dummies at Fayid and claimed the destruction of nine aircraft: eight MiGs and one transport. During egress, the HAT Ouragans strafed Egyptian military vehicles along roads in Sinai.

Mission 117/5, ERIKA, departed Ramat David at 0727hrs tasked to bomb targets 1 and 2 along Abu Sueir runway 09/27. The four Mirages claimed destruction of ten Il-28s and four or five MiG-21s. A minute after ERIKA took off, at 0728hrs Mission 113/8 (callsign APRON) departed Khatsor tasked to bomb targets 1 and 2 along Bir Gafgafa runway 15/33. APRON reported that four bombs and 25 rockets hit the runway. Nevertheless, a MiG-21 was seen to take off from Bir Gafgafa during APRON's attack, but it did not engage the Ouragans. APRON reported the destruction of four aircraft on the ground as well as the presence of dummy MiG-19s at the south side of the airfield. Antiaircraft fire hit APRON 4; the damaged aircraft and injured pilot did not fly again until after the war.

Mission 105/8 departed Khatsor at 0730hrs tasked to bomb targets 1 and 2 along Kabrit runway 13/31. LATIF's bombing hits were not observed. LATIF 2 encountered a MiG-17 that was flying with undercarriage down and initiated an attack, upon which the MiG was seen to activate afterburner, climb and turn, but with the undercarriage still down. LATIF 2

CURTAIN for Cairo West: 0750hrs

Only two Mirage formations attacked enemy air bases with runway-piercing bombs on June 5, 1967: Mission 101/4 tasked to strike Cairo West from 0810hrs and Mission 101/9 that attacked Helwan from around 1120hrs.

Squadron 101 had been qualified with the heavier runway-piercing bomb – Olar Khad – a short while before the outbreak of the war. The Squadron 101 configuration with runway-piercing bombs seems to have been two 250kg bombs in tandem under the fuselage, two fuel tanks fitted to the inner wing stations, and two Olar Khad bombs loaded onto the outer wing stations. While Mirages usually dive-bombed and then strafed, the Mirage missions tasked to strike with runway-piercing bombs first dive-bombed, returned to fly at low altitude along the runway to drop the runway-piercing bombs, and then returned to strafe.

The 22 Mirages dropped 36 500kg bombs, eight 250kg bombs, and eight Olar Khad heavier runway-piercing bombs on Cairo West. The first formation – CURTAIN – claimed the destruction of eight Tu-16s, three Il-28s, and three MiG-21s, while AIR4 evaluated that CURTAIN destroyed a total of ten aircraft. The destruction of 19–31 percent of the stationed aircraft generated smoke that complicated the strike for following formations. AIR1 History indicated that the combined claim of the six Mirage formations that raided Cairo West during FOCUS first wave was 11 Tu-16s, eight MiG-21s, five Il-28s, and five MiG-15/17s for a total of 29 aircraft claimed as destroyed, or 56 percent of the AIR4 evaluation of 52 combat aircraft stationed at Cairo West on June 5, 1967. None of the attacking Mirages was lost.

fired on the MiG-17 and noted flames erupting from its engine and left wing. The MiG-17 rolled over, LATIF 2 disengaged, and LATIF 1 reported seeing the MiG crash, confirming the kill. LATIF reported at least 12 MiGs burning on the ground at Kabrit, but LATIF's reporting standard was so poor that it is unclear if the reference is to LATIF's claim or to the overall situation at Kabrit.

Just 20 minutes after the first formation took off, Mission 107/2 departed Lod at 0734hrs. It was tasked to attack AAA emplacements with rockets as the second and final *Focus* formation to raid El Arish. Antiaircraft fire damaged the lead Ouragan and injured the leader. Number 3 Iftach Sadan took command and the three Ouragans flew two strafing passes each, claiming one damaged aircraft; URTICA had already destroyed all active aircraft at El Arish. Meanwhile, the leader flew to Lod, orbited overhead until the three Ouragans returned from El Arish, and then landed. The damaged Ouragan was quickly repaired and flew again the following day, but the injured pilot's career as a fighter pilot was over.

Striking radar stations and search-and-rescue

Fourteen *Focus* formations had hit their targets within ten minutes of H-Hour. Tactical surprise had been accomplished. The formations were not detected during ingress,[7] the EAF did not scramble interceptors prior to H-Hour, and after H-Hour it was too late: within minutes, many runways had been cratered and the destruction of aircraft on the ground was ongoing. The first formations to strafe usually accomplished the lion's share of destruction. They encountered fewer obstructions than later strikes, since antiaircraft fire probably improved during *Focus*, while smoke from burning aircraft degraded the effectiveness of spotting and strafing.

The first 14 formations reported the destruction of up to 120 aircraft on the ground plus five in the air for the loss of only five aircraft. At El Arish, all EAF aircraft present had been destroyed. At Bir Tamada, most of the stationed EAF aircraft had been destroyed. Three MiG-21s were seen to escape from Bir Gafgafa, but most other EAF aircraft present at Bir Gafgafa had been destroyed. At Abu Sueir, Fayid, and Kabrit, up to 59 aircraft had been

7   Despite claims that the Jordanian radar station at Ajloun detected the IAF departures, and reported this to the Egyptian officer in command of the Jordanian armed forces who telegrammed a message from Amman to Cairo as early as 0725hrs, it is highly unlikely that a 1960s state-of-the-art radar station was able to detect very low-flying aircraft at a range of over 100km. For example, a contemporary P-20 radar could detect a fighter-size aircraft at 18,000ft at up to 200km, but detection range dropped dramatically with altitude so that with the aircraft at 1,000ft the detection range was only up to 30km.

A gunsight view from a Mirage strafing, from west to east, the line between Cairo West runways 28 and 34. Tu-16 number 14 is closest and Tu-16 number 06 or 08 farthest away, the latter most likely armed with AS-1 missiles. Squadron 101's CURTAIN that attacked Cairo West from 0750hrs claimed destruction on the ground of eight Tu-16s. (AC)

reported as destroyed by the five strafing formations, out of an AIR4 evaluation of 141 stationed aircraft. The first (and only) formations at that time to raid Cairo West and Inchas reported the destruction of up to 14 and 15 aircraft respectively.

Radio silence was lifted after H-Hour, but low flying continued when necessary to evade radar stations and SA-2 batteries. From 0747 to 0808hrs, four Fouga four-ship formations departed Khatserim tasked to attack Egyptian radar stations in Sinai. At 0800hrs, a Nord departed Ekron to patrol over the Mediterranean Sea, picking up transmissions from pilots who had ejected. Around that time an S-58 helicopter was scrambled from Ekron to search for SWEATHER 2, who had ejected over the Mediterranean, but the two-hour search yielded no result; the pilot had been fished out by Egyptian boats, handed over to the authorities, and ended Mission 113/1 as a prisoner of war.

Time Over Target 0800hrs

Three formations were tasked to strike Bir Tamada, Inchas, and Cairo West from 0800hrs. Most aircraft stationed at Bir Tamada had been destroyed, so the base had been practically wiped out as a functioning military unit. Inchas and Cairo West had been attacked by one formation each from 0750hrs and sustained significant damage. Nominally, there were at Inchas and Cairo West at least around 20 and ten MiG-21s respectively that escaped damage during the first wave. However, it is reasonable to assume that APARTMENT and CURTAIN had damaged or destroyed some or even all of the MiG-21s that were supposed to be on readiness. Neither Inchas nor Cairo West seem to have scrambled MiG-21s to face *Focus* formations that attacked from 0750hrs and from 0800hrs.

Bir Tamada runway 18/30 had already been bombed by SHELF on Mission 101/7 and by LILIUM on Mission 107/4. The Mystères of Mission 109/4, callsign COTTON, took off from Ramat David at 0723hrs to hit it again. COTTON counted at least ten aircraft burning on the ground prior to strafing the only seemingly intact aircraft: two MiG-17s and one Il-14.

Mission 119/6 left Ekron at 0727hrs tasked to bomb targets 1 and 3 on Cairo West runway 10/28. Smoke from burning aircraft – especially the fuel-laden Tu-16s, which generated considerably more black smoke than fighters – was a nuisance that obscured aiming points during bombing runs and made spotting for targets during strafing passes difficult. LINTEL claimed the destruction of a bomber – either a Tu-16 as reported by LINTEL 1 or an Il-28 as reported by LINTEL 3 – plus two MiG-21s and two MiG-17 dummies.

Lastly in this wave, Mission 105/1 departed Khatsor at 0733hrs tasked to bomb targets 1 and 3 along Inchas runway 09/27. DUBEK reported that two bombs hit target 1. DUBEK 3 crashed during the strike and antiaircraft fire damaged DUBEK 1. Strafing yielded a claim for three or four MiG-21s either damaged or destroyed; the reporting standard was so poor that it is unclear if the number of claims were three or four and if the claim was damage or destruction.

The three formations that attacked from 0800hrs claimed the destruction on the ground of up to ten aircraft for the loss of one of their own. The average claim of the first seven formations to strafe was more than ten aircraft destroyed on the ground per formation.

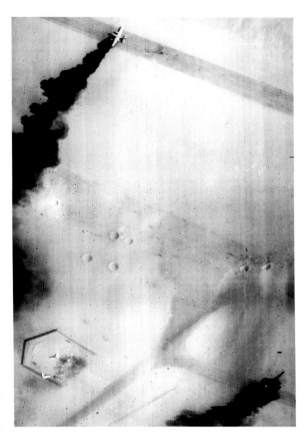

AIR4 did not evaluate that Il-28s were at Cairo West on June 5, yet CURTAIN claimed three Il-28s destroyed, while LINTEL reported destroying a bomber, either an Il-28 or Tu-16. In this photograph of runway 10/28, by GUTTER 4 sometime after 0855hrs, can be seen an Il-28 on the taxiway, a destroyed Tu-16 in a pen, a burning bomber – probably a Tu-16 – and seven craters around target 3, including two misses, possibly resulting from the northerly crosswind – as can be deduced from the smoke. (AC)

The five formations that attacked from 0755hrs claimed an average destruction on the ground of eight aircraft, while the three formations that attacked from 0800hrs averaged three claims of enemy aircraft destroyed on the ground per formation.

Fifteen minutes after H-Hour, 17 formations had raided eight EAF bases. All of the 17 *Focus* strike formations attacked as planned, and claimed destruction of up to 130 aircraft on the ground plus five aircraft in the air for the loss of six aircraft. The claim-to-loss ratio was thus 22.5 claims per loss, a ratio that can hardly be matched in any other type of air campaign.

The AIR4 evaluation of the EAF's deployment and inventory prior to *Focus* H-Hour listed 260 combat aircraft stationed in the eight bases that had now been attacked. Within slightly more than 15 minutes, the IAF had practically destroyed many, if not all, of the EAF combat units stationed in these eight bases, while there were still 28 *Focus* formations planned to strike during the first wave in order to top off destruction of the EAF.

It was at around this time – minutes after 0800hrs – that the combined team of AIR2 and AIR4, which had been collecting claims and reports in order to feed a proper picture of the current situation to AIR3 planners, started to issue an initial evaluation of *Focus*'s success so far. Postwar, IAF Commander Moti Hod recalled:

> There was the matter of bombing Tel Aviv and this was an issue that repeatedly surfaced from May 15 [1967] until June 5 [1967]. It was discussed on a daily basis including [Prime Minister Levy] Eshkol asking me, at least twice, during IDF General Staff meetings, whether we can guarantee that Tel Aviv would not be bombed. I answered "I can guarantee that Tel Aviv would not be ruined but it may suffer a few bombings. If citizens will be in shelters then the only damage will be a few ruined buildings. It is impossible to promise that no bombs will be dropped on Tel Aviv but if we will destroy the [Egyptian] bombers then Tel Aviv will not be the subject of air raids."
>
> The fact that only Egypt fielded bombers and the pressure [to remove the threat of bombings] against Tel Aviv eased my decision to concentrate our effort [against Egypt] so that Tel Aviv would not be bombed… I started to receive battle damage reports at 0815hrs. Strikes started at 0745hrs; at about 0805hrs, 0810hrs we started to receive reports from the air and we wrote off every bomber, one by one, until we arrived at 100 percent, until we were sure that all bombers had been destroyed.

The smoking remains of Tu-16 number 14 and Tu-16 number 06 or 08 on the third spot from left and second spot from right along the line between runways 28 and 34 at Cairo West. (AC)

Time Over Target 0810hrs

The constraints that affected planning of the first *Focus* strikes – radio silence, low flying, offensive patrols, and coastline crossings – had been practically lifted. The next *Focus* formations attacked in line with prewar planning at 15-minute intervals until – after three 15-minute intervals – the IAF had almost run out of available aircraft; those that had already returned were starting to finish turnaround in order to begin the second wave.

Unable to fly a low-altitude ingress from Ramat David to Beni Suef, TIGRIS had deployed from Ramat David to Ekron during the late afternoon hours of June 4. TIGRIS departed Ekron at 0717hrs, with eight 70kg bombs per Vautour, tasked to strike targets 1 and 2 along Beni Suef runway 01/19. Surprise at Beni Suef was compromised in order to secure surprise over the six closer air bases to be attacked at H-Hour and the two Nile Delta air bases to be attacked from 0750hrs. However, the IAF expected the 25 minutes' delay to be significantly less than the reaction time of the EAF bomber force. Flying Mission 110/1 as TIGRIS 4, Herzle Bodinger recalled:

We were told during briefing that the future of the State of Israel was dependent upon the success of *Focus*. Preservation of surprise was emphasized. We had two radio sets – formation channel and control channel – and one of these was switched OFF while the other was switched ON in case of 'abort mission' message but the transmission selector was switched to the OFF radio set ensuring that accidental clicks would not violate the electromagnetic silence.

The canopy of [TIGRIS 2] Giora Goren's Vautour failed to lock and we could not wait until the maintainers would fix the problem, we had to depart right on time so we departed as a three-ship formation. We flew very low, south and over Khatserim we saw the deception Fouga trainers. When we crossed the border I realized that it was real and shortly after crossing the border we flew over an Egyptian military convoy. The Egyptian soldiers waved at us and this filled me with joy; surprise has been accomplished. We flew in the direction of Bir Tamada where we turned, crossed the Gulf of Suez and flew into a huge canyon that was to lead us right to the target.

As we approached [the] River Nile, morning mists began to cover the sky from 700ft above ground level so we flew under a canopy of a thin layer of clouds. This was a worrying phenomenon as we had to climb, to visually acquire the target and to dive bomb… but the Egyptians did not construct air bases on land that could be cultivated as this was a rare resource in a mostly desert nation so Beni Suef was located in the dunes further inland beyond the edge of the rural area. As a result, the morning mist was mostly over the humid cultivated land but not over the dry dunes. We climbed and there it was, spread out in front of us. A new large air base with long wide runways and the aircraft were parked in open pens.

We flew the first bombing run and got all the bombs right on target and so it was during the second bombing run as well, I was trailing behind so I saw the hits of the first two aircraft in front of me. The bombs were set to explode 7–15 seconds after hitting the surface so that all aircraft would clear the area before the explosions. I saw the holes of the hits ahead of me and the explosions when I looked back over my shoulder.

We then flew three strafing passes. The Vautour's 30mm cannon pack covered an area as large as 20 meters wide and 20 meters long. During training we only fired the lower right cannon that had the central aiming point with the aiming points of the remaining three cannon scattered around but during the war we fired all four cannon for the first time. We just could not miss such a large target as a Tu-16 and each one of us destroyed one bomber in every strafing pass. We were three aircraft and we flew three passes so we destroyed nine Tu-16s. We disengaged but flew east at low level, an SA-2 battery was located south of the air base. The SA-2 was not effective against aircraft flying lower than 3,000ft and most of the time we were really low. We climbed to 6,000ft only during pop up so we endeavored that the

TIGRIS at Beni Suef: 0810hrs

Three Squadron 110 Vautour formations attacked Beni Suef on June 5, 1967: Mission 110/1 TIGRIS from 0810hrs, Mission 110/2 JORDAN from 0825hrs, and Mission 110/3 VISTULA from 0855hrs. The Vautours' strike pattern included two bombing runs – dropping four 70kg bombs on the runways in each – followed by several strafing passes. Armed with four 30mm cannon, the hitting power of a Vautour strafing parked aircraft was devastating.

TIGRIS and JORDAN destroyed all the Tu-16s at Beni Suef. TIGRIS claimed the destruction of nine Tu-16s, while JORDAN claimed destruction of seven Tu-16s. The two following formations were unable to pinpoint intact Tu-16s for strafing. VISTULA 1 photographed Beni Suef to confirm the destructions. AIR4 concluded that ten Tu-16s were destroyed at Beni Suef during the FOCUS first wave. AIR3 did not issue any more mission orders to strike Beni Suef.

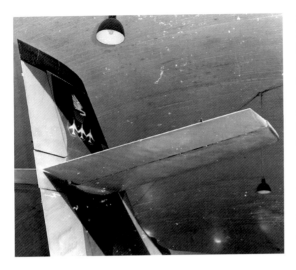

Each of the three Squadron 110 TIGRIS Vautours that flew Mission 110/1 to strike Beni Suef from 0825hrs claimed the destruction of three Tu-16s. (ARC)

timeframe we flew higher than 3,000 feet would be limited to less than 30 seconds. They launched a surface-to-air missile but it did not lock on to us. By the time we climbed we began to hear reports from other formations and it was crystal clear that we succeeded though losses were indeed sustained.

During disengagement I also suffered an electrical trim control malfunction and I had to fly slower, I never enquired into it so I do not know if I got hit but I reported to my leader and I managed to fly all the way to Ramat David.

Five out of eight formations tasked to attack at 0810hrs were armed with runway-piercing bombs, including Mission 109/3, which departed Ramat David at 0734hrs to strike Bir Gafgafa's runway 15/33. Antiaircraft fire hit CONCRETE 2 and 3 during the relatively risky runway-piercing bomb delivery pattern, but both pressed on with the attack. CONCRETE 4's runway-piercing bombs failed to drop, a not uncommon occurrence at the time when the weapon was still new. CONCRETE flew two strafing passes and claimed three MiG-21s and four Mi-6s. During egress, CONCRETE 1 ordered CONCRETE 2 and 4 to press the panic button that jettisoned all external loads, so that CONCRETE 4 would get rid of its hung-up runway-piercing bombs and the damaged CONCRETE 2 would be able to make it to Ramat David. The two wingmen landed first, and then CONCRETE 1 escorted CONCRETE 3 to land Mystère 26 without a functioning airspeed indicator owing to damage to the pitot tube; the drill was that the escorting aircraft flew the landing pattern beside the damaged aircraft so that the speed of the damaged aircraft would be correct for landing. When the damaged aircraft was on final approach and was about to land on the runway, the escorting aircraft turned away to fly its own landing circuit while the damaged aircraft continued straight ahead and finished its landing. Post-landing examination revealed that Mystère 26's pitot tube was torn away, and the air intake, the leading edge of the right wing, and the elevator were all damaged. However, the Mystère was flying again on the night of June 5–6. CONCRETE 2's Mystère 11 returned with two large holes in the left wing. The wing had to be replaced so the Mystère was grounded until June 8.

Mission 101/4 departed Khatsor at 0737hrs tasked to bomb targets 1 and 3 along Cairo West runway 10/28 with, probably, two 250kg bombs and two heavier runway-piercing bombs per aircraft. The first *Focus* task assignment program of March 16 had tasked Mission 101/4 to bomb with two 500kg bombs per Mirage, but the final version tasked it to attack with runway-piercing bombs owing to the Mirage's qualification, obtained after March 16, to drop the heavier Olar Khad[8] runway-piercing bombs.

FAUTEUIL 2 strafed the control tower and a parking place that was covered with a camouflage net and may have hosted two MiG-17s. FAUTEUIL 3 reported destruction of a MiG-21, while FAUTEUIL 4 claimed destruction of two Tu-16s, including one that did not explode. FAUTEUIL 1 diverted to land at Khatserim, while the other three FAUTEUIL pilots returned to Khatsor.

Mission 116/3 departed Ekron at 0740hrs tasked to strike targets 1 and 2 along Fayid runway 09/27 with six light runway-piercing bombs per aircraft. GANDHI 4 reported a fuel

8   IAF called the original lighter runway-piercing bomb PPM – pronounced Pa-pam – for the acronym in Hebrew of runway-piercing bomb; the IAF name for the heavier runway-piercing bombs was Olar Khad, pronounced O-lar Khad; it means Sharp Pocketknife.

problem immediately after the bombing run; one of the two 625-liter (165 gallons) external fuel tanks of Mystère 85 failed to feed, so GANDHI 1 ordered GANDHI 4 to abort mission and to return to base alone. GANDHI 4 landed at Khatserim. GANDHI 1's target during the first strafing pass was a transport that he described as a Vickers Viscount in a commercial-style scheme. Egyptian fighter pilot Samir Aziz Michail, who was at Fayid during the attack, said: "At this point an Il-14 landed which had the vice president… on board. All those on the plane ran out when it stopped. After that it was strafed and caught fire." Perhaps this Il-14 was the transport aircraft that GANDHI 1 had attacked.

In his second strafing pass, GANDHI 1 claimed a MiG-19 destroyed. In his third strafing pass, the Squadron 116 Commander strafed a MiG-17 that exploded in a huge fireball, its debris damaging the strafing Mystère. GANDHI 1 turned east, climbed, jettisoned the canopy since the cockpit was full of smoke, and crossed the Suez Canal as it headed back east, but an explosion rocked the aircraft and Jonathan Shahar ejected from Mystère 45 at an altitude of 5,000ft into a seemingly peaceful scene, except for the pilotless jet fighter trailing a huge blaze of fire. GANDHI 3 assumed command, noted Shahar's location, shepherded GANDHI 2 back to Ekron, and reported the destruction of four MiG-21s, a Sukhoi, and a Viscount, while postwar Squadron 116 reported the destruction of six fighters and one Antonov transport aircraft. These reports probably excluded the MiG-17 and MiG-19 that Shahar strafed during his second and third passes.

Mission 105/4 departed Khatsor at 0740hrs tasked to attack targets 1 and 2 along Inchas runway 04/22 with light runway-piercing bombs. The strike suffered multiple hang-ups of their runway-piercing bombs: three from PRESIDENT 1, one from PRESIDENT 3, and all six from PRESIDENT 4. PRESIDENT reported sighting of seven to eight damaged MiGs on the ground, but the reporting standard was so poor that it is unclear if these sightings resulted from PRESIDENT's actions or from those of preceding formations. During egress, PRESIDENT pilots saw an Il-14 flying in the vicinity of Ismailia.

Mission 105/2 departed Khatsor at 0742hrs tasked to attack targets 1 and 2 on Abu Sueir runway 09/27 with light runway-piercing bombs. At the time flying as PERFECT 4, Oded Flum later recalled:

Each one of us hauled six runway-piercing bombs and we had to fly along the runway axis from west to east at precisely 300ft above ground level and 400 knots. Just as we entered

FAR LEFT
AIR3 Offense Section Chief Yossi Sarig, right, was in charge of planning Operation *Focus*. He is photographed postwar at Bir Gafgafa, examining a crater that was probably caused by a runway-piercing bomb, with AIR2 Ordnance Section Chief Joseph Afik and the Ordnance Section Chief of MAT5, the fifth branch of the IAF Material Department. If this crater was indeed the result of a runway-piercing bomb, it was dropped by Squadron 109's COTTON flying Mission 109/3. (AC)

LEFT
The Squadron 116 Commander Jonathan Shahar – photographed in the briefing room – ejected from his Mystère east of Fayid at around 0820hrs, evaded capture, and was rescued by a Super Frelon that night. His younger brother Meir, a Squadron 117 Mirage pilot, flew his second mission from 1258hrs and his third from 1515hrs, but was killed when his Mirage crashed at around 1540hrs. Postwar, IAF History and AIR1 Statistics credited him with a MiG-21 kill before he was shot down. (AC)

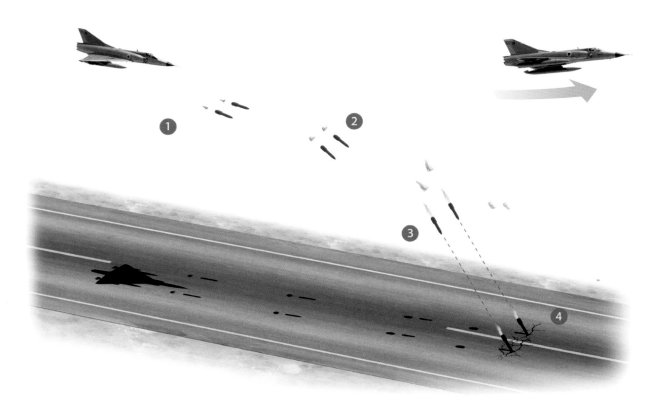

ABOVE: RUNWAY-PIERCING BOMB DELIVERY

The runway-piercing bomb delivery pattern resembled a napalm strike flight profile, rather than the usual IAF runway attack pattern of pop up, roll over, dive, and release bombs. In a runway-piercing bomb strike, the attacking aircraft flew low and fast along the runway. Dropped from the aircraft at an altitude of 300ft, the runway-piercing bomb then deployed a parachute that slowed it down, increasing separation between aircraft and bomb and helping ensure that the explosion would not damage the aircraft. When the bomb pointed down, at 60 degrees to the runway surface, a rocket ignited. The bomb accelerated, penetrated the runway and, after six seconds, exploded deeper than a regular bomb, so that a small warhead created a relatively large crater – up to 5m in diameter and 1.6m deep – that would take more effort to repair. Israel Military Industries delivered to the IAF only 187 PPM (light) and 66 Olar Khad (heavy) runway-piercing bombs during 1966. Only Squadron 101 Mirages were qualified to carry Olar Khads, in a configuration that included one Olar Khad bomb loaded onto each of the outer wing stations.

our bombing run I saw two MiG-21s head-on but everybody ignored them. I concentrated in my aiming, released the bombs and nothing happened. After I landed it turned out that only a single bomb was dropped; the improvised mechanism to release the runway-piercing bombs was to turn the rocket selector to 12, turn on a safety switch and release the bombs, but it failed.

We then had to fly three strafing passes. During our first strafing pass I saw the two MiG-21s pull up to get organized for an attack against us. The AAA fired upwards but during our second pass I noticed "AAA" firing downwards, it was a MiG-21 flying 300–400 meters behind [PERFECT 3 Ben-Zion] Gaifman and shooting. The radio channel was fully occupied and I was not able to report anything. Moreover, we were still flying with large

1,300-liter [340-gallon] external fuel tanks that were still feeding fuel. We were ordered to do our best not to jettison fuel tanks as these were in short supply. I decided to chase that MiG so I pushed the panic button to release all external stores but again nothing happened. I pointed my shivering Super Mystère at the MiG but he pulled up to 6,000ft and ejected. I leveled my heavy Super Mystère and the same thing happened with the other MiG-21, he pulled up and ejected.

PERFECT 1 called off the attack after one strafing pass, and PERFECT 2 reported that the formation had destroyed four aircraft on the ground but did not specify the types of aircraft claimed as destroyed.

Mission 113/6 departed Khatsor at 0745hrs tasked to attack targets 1 and 2 along Bir Tamada runway 12/30. SHIRT departed at H-Hour, so it was the first *Focus* formation to fly to its target at a higher altitude and not under radio silence. The Ouragans bombed targets 1 and 2 as planned and then hit target 3 with rockets, but there were no intact aircraft on the ground for strafing. SHIRT 1 reported scattered antiaircraft fire, while SHIRT 3 reported intensive antiaircraft fire, which holed an Ouragan 70 wingtip fuel tank. Overall, SHIRT reported that Bir Tamada had been suppressed and that all aircraft stationed there had been destroyed.

As Squadron 105 was running out of serviceable Super Mystères after committing eight full four-ship formations, Mission 105/9 would be a three-ship formation. Callsign EDEN, it departed Khatsor at 0748hrs tasked to bomb targets 3 and 4 along Kabrit runway 18/36. Kabrit was covered with smoke, so EDEN 1 did not see where its bombs hit, while the hits of EDEN 2 were reported as 100m overshot in the center of the runways, and those of EDEN 3 were not reported at all. Reporting of strafing results was similarly confusing: EDEN 2 hit a MiG in every pass, while EDEN 3 was sure of having hit two MiGs, but the number of strafing passes was not reported! Separately, EDEN 1 indicated three strafing passes and a personal claim for two MiGs and one Mi-6, so the total EDEN claim was possibly up to seven MiGs – most likely all MiG-15/17s – and one helicopter.

The eight formations that attacked from 0810hrs added claims for up to 40 aircraft destroyed on the ground plus two MiG-21s in the air at the cost of one Mystère, while one of the Fouga armed trainers tasked to attack radar stations in Sinai was lost during egress,

The Squadron 113 Ouragans that flew Mission 113/6 to strike Bir Tamada from 0810hrs were armed with two 250kg bombs and eight T-10 rockets. This Ouragan is similarly configured. In ideal conditions, the 250kg bombs produced a runway crater 8m across and 2m deep, while the T-10 rocket produced a 1.5m crater 40cm deep. (AC)

shortly after 0810hrs. The total claim of the first 25 *Focus* strike formations amounted to up to 170 aircraft destroyed on the ground plus seven aircraft in the air for the loss of eight aircraft. The claim-to-loss ratio was down to 21-to-1, but even allowing for over-optimistic reports, it was clear that within just over 30 minutes of H-Hour, the *Focus* objectives had already been achieved.

Time Over Target 0825hrs

From 0825hrs, eight formations were tasked to raid the same eight EAF bases that had been attacked from 0810hrs. By then the IDF had initiated the parallel ground offensive, and at 0817hrs the first Fouga formation tasked to support IDF Command South Division 84 departed Khatserim to attack Egyptian artillery in northeast Sinai.

EAF aerial opposition had been negligible and limited to Egyptian territory, while there were no signs of unusual activity from the JAF and SAF. Still, the first two of the six Mirage pairs held back on alert were scrambled: Mission 101/1 from Khatsor at 0808hrs to patrol over Sinai and Mission 117/1 from Ramat David at 0820hrs to patrol over northern Israel.

The first to take off was Mission 110/2, which departed Ramat David at 0725hrs tasked to bomb targets 1 and 2 along Beni Suef runway 01/19 at 0825hrs. It departed only eight minutes after Mission 110/1 (which attacked Beni Suef from 0810hrs) because the two formations flew different mission profiles. TIGRIS flew at low altitude all the way to Beni Suef. JORDAN started at low altitude, then exactly at H-Hour, 0745hrs, they climbed to the more efficient cruise altitude and descended back to low altitude before the attack. For this reason the second Vautour formation to raid Beni Suef had enough fuel to fly the mission from Ramat David, while the first had to depart from Ekron. SA-2s and smoke challenged and complicated JORDAN's strike, but the Vautours ended the attack with seven Tu-16s claimed destroyed.

Next to go was Mission 110/4, which departed Ramat David at 0749hrs tasked to bomb targets 1 and 3 along Abu Sueir runway 04/22, as well as to strike an SA-2 battery in the Port Said sector during egress, while the lead Vautour IIN was equipped with cameras and therefore also tasked to take photos. Originally, the mission was to be flown by a five-

Four Fouga armed trainers flying over IDF Command South troops en route to strike Egyptian forces in Sinai. Throughout June 5, Squadron 147 supported Command South, but in order to mitigate the pressure upon AIR3 it had been agreed that until *Focus* was complete, Command South would issue improvised mission orders directly to Squadron 147 over a point-to-point phone from Beer Sheba to Khatserim. (ILGP/PO)

ship formation, including a Vautour IIB reconnaissance bomber. Hauling bombs but lacking cannon, the Vautour IIB was to bomb Abu Sueir, then collect battle damage assessment (BDA) images of the air base during the strafing passes of the other Vautours. However, the IAF had only two Vautour IIB reconnaissance bombers. The original *Focus* first-wave BDA effort included a Mirage mission to photograph the Nile Delta and Suez Canal air bases, with the other Vautour IIB tasked to photograph the closer Sinai air bases. In the final *Focus* task assignment program, the Abu Sueir Vautour IIB was reassigned to fly the Beni Suef mission as neither of the two planned BDA missions was planned to cover that base. Flying Mission 110/4 as BANIAS 3, Beni Zohar recalled:

Five Il-28s still intact at Abu Sueir, along the westernmost "eights" dispersal, with a sixth already burning. The first three formations to strafe Abu Sueir – from 0755hrs, 0810hrs, and 0825hrs – claimed destruction of about half of the Il-28s that were present at Abu Sueir. (AC)

[Ramat David Wing 1 Commander Ezekiel] Somech briefed all aircrews a day before the war. He did not say "there will be a war tomorrow" but he presented guidelines. We had to depart in radio silence, a pretty complicated procedure that we could not practice as this would have revealed our secret so we only practiced it by taxiing. He [Somech] told us that during the war we should not pay attention to our personal safety or to the safety of the aircraft. For example, if a pilot experienced a malfunction during the radio-silence departure he should do everything to keep the runway operational even at the risk of being killed. We assumed that we would suffer 20–30 percent losses during the first wave. Again, his guideline was not to pay attention to risks but to press on with the mission regardless of consequences.

My first mission was to Abu Sueir. We came in low and as we climbed I saw additional aircraft trailing us. We knew that there was a possibility that Mirages would fly a patrol to protect us. At first glance I thought that these were Mirages but then I saw, 1,000–1,500m ahead, an air-to-air missile. I could actually see its spiral trajectory chasing the leading pair that was diving to bomb but it was crystal clear that this air-to-air missile could not harm them. Only then did I realize that these aircraft were MiG-21s, not Mirages, so to comply with [Somech's] briefing I had to do everything to ensure that the attack would be pressed on, [so] at least three of us would attack.

I transmitted over the radio that I was engaging the MiG-21s. They came in a not very threatening manner, more or less at our speed, a little faster. They slowly closed on us with the two pairs trailing each other rather than splitting, activating their afterburners and chasing us; it actually resembled an escort!

I ordered my wingman to bomb and I started to turn. If they had followed the bombers I would have followed them but all four of them followed me, turning. Not a single one of them really threatened me; I did not even jettison my bombs. They were not turning very well and I observed all the mess down there at the air base: smoke from previous air raids,

PERFECT MiG encounter at Abu Sueir: 0810hrs

The four Super Mystères of PERFECT flight have bombed Abu Sueir runway at low level (300ft) and broken into the 270 strike pattern. A pair of MiG-21s dived on the strafing Super Mystères, fired on them, and then zoom-climbed to escape. When the pilot of the MiG reached 6,000ft, he ejected from his aircraft over Abu Sueir.

One Super Mystère failed to drop five of its small runway-piercing bombs. When the MiGs passed over, the pilot raised its nose to point at the MiGs, but was easily outpaced.

dust from the ongoing attack. I had to get rid of the bombs but why jettison the bombs without a purpose?

I lowered my nose, entered the smoke but as I exited the smoke I noticed that I was between the runways, [and] there was nothing I could do [to correct the bombing run]. I released the bombs, climbed back and then I saw only three [MiG-21s]. I reported that I was mixing it with only three and that the fourth was with the strikers; he bothered them a little, they threatened him and he disengaged. I turned with the MiG-21s so the other Vautours could bomb and strafe according to plan, albeit in a three-ship formation.

They reported "we are going home" and only then I noticed that I had a fuel problem. One of the 1,200kg belly tanks did not feed fuel, I was stuck with that weight; I could not drop it, I could not use it.

I disengaged when I was in a 90 degrees advantage over one MiG and the pair were 180 degrees from me. If I had time and fuel I might have shot him down, but this was not the case and during the turn, when I was heading towards Ismailia, I simply dropped my nose and dived from about 6,000, 8,000 or 10,000ft. I did not even look back at them; as an agricultural pilot I simply shaved the earth.

I regrouped with the formation and as we crossed the coastline we strafed an SA-2 battery. I thought that we had to damage the battery because soon I would have to climb. Up to an altitude of 2,000ft we were pretty safe and below 5,000ft the SA-2 was not very effective but I had to climb to preserve fuel. The others continued a little longer at low altitude just in case but I climbed immediately. I shut down one engine, left the other at full power and it kept me going at 30,000ft. I figured that I would have to eject over the sea but the closer [to Israel] the better. Then I reached a point where I figured that if I would switch off both engines and glide, there was a chance that I might land. I was permitted direct approach, I restarted one engine but I left it on idle just in case and I landed.

[Those] in the Hardened Aircraft Shelter told me that when I came down they could not understand me, they only heard "missile… fighters… air combat… fuel… one engine" and although I do not remember that I was so excited, we actually returned from a mission from which we thought that we would not return alive.

A MiG-17 burning at Bir Tamada. The three adjacent black stains may have been MiG-17s. By the time of the ROSE strike from 0825hrs, there were no more targets to strafe at Bir Tamada. (AC)

Tasked to attack Bir Tamada, Mission 107/3 departed Lod at 0751hrs, but Bir Tamada was practically suppressed, with most if not all stationed aircraft destroyed, so ROSE – flying as a three-ship formation because Squadron 107 was relatively short of aircraft – instead strafed ground forces north and northeast of Bir Tamada.

Mission 101/5 took off from Khatsor at 0753hrs tasked to bomb targets 1 and 2 along Cairo West runway 18/34. DESKTOP reported all bombs on target, a lot of smoke over Cairo West, and seemingly no AAA fire. DESKTOP 1 reported definite hits on two Tu-16s plus possible hits on one more, and DESKTOP 3 reported hits on three Tu-16s for a total claim of up to five Tu-16s.

SULPHUR was the third and final first-wave formation to bomb Kabrit's runway 13/31, hitting targets 1 and 2. Mission 109/1 departed Ekron at 0754hrs. To complicate the enemy's battle damage repair effort and to bridge the gap until resumption of the attack during the expected second wave, some of SULPHUR's bombs had one-hour delay fuses set to explode at 0925hrs.

Mission 113/5 departed Khatsor at 0755hrs tasked to attack target 1 on Fayid runway 09/27 and target 3 along runway 18/36. FUR reported severe smoke over Fayid,

Prewar, the IAF evaluated that the aircraft at Jabel Libni were not operational. *Flight* magazine reported afterwards that two MiG-17s were destroyed here while on QRA, connected to battery carts. However, since the strike at Jabel Libni began some 40 minutes after H-Hour, if these two MiG-17s were indeed on readiness, why were they still waiting to take off? (AC)

with at least five aircraft still burning on the ground. FUR 1, 2, and 3 bombed target 1, FUR 4 hit target 2, and all four aircraft struck target 3 with rockets, but FUR did not report destruction of aircraft on the ground.

At 0758hrs, Mission 105/5 also departed Khatsor to attack targets 1 and 2 on Inchas runway 04/22. MENTHOL 3 aborted the mission and returned to base. MENTHOL pressed ahead but did not attack Inchas. The three Super Mystères bombed another airfield's runway but did not strafe; Squadron 105 reported that the bombed airfield was Cairo International Airport.

The last of the 0825hrs raids was Mission 113/3, which took off from Khatsor at 0802hrs to attack targets 1 and 2 on Bir Gafgafa runway 33. TROUSER reported many aircraft burning on the ground and claimed one MiG-21 either damaged or destroyed.

Also attacking an EAF base during this period were the two Mission 117/7 Mirages escorting the Mission 110/6 Vautours that were flying an electronic warfare mission to jam Egyptian SA-2 batteries, all of which left Ramat David at 0721hrs. Eventually, the Mission 117/7 Mirages were vectored to intercept enemy aircraft that turned out to be IAF Ouragans returning from a *Focus* mission. The Mission 117/7 Mirages were then tasked to strafe Jabel Libni airfield in Sinai. The Mirage pilots reported destruction of all aircraft observed at Jabel Libni: four MiG-17s destroyed, plus a MiG-17 that was damaged and was most likely a dummy. AIR4 evaluated that the aircraft at Jabel Libni were MiGs withdrawn from active service and used as decoys, and this was probably the case.

The formations that attacked at 0825hrs claimed no more than 13 aircraft destroyed, but that figure included up to 12 Tu-16s. The total claim of the first 33 *Focus* strike formations had risen to up to 183 aircraft destroyed on the ground, plus seven in the air, for the loss of eight aircraft.

Time Over Target 0840hrs

From 0840hrs, seven formations were tasked to raid the same EAF bases that had been attacked from 0810hrs and 0825hrs, except Bir Tamada. By then – from 0825 to 0840hrs – the first *Focus* BDA mission had departed and Squadron 147 dispatched one more Fouga formation tasked to support IDF Command South Division 84 by attacking Egyptian artillery in northeast Sinai.

Squadron 110's RIVER 275 departed Ramat David at 0829hrs to photograph Bir Gafgafa and Bir Tamada. This photograph, showing the silhouette of the reconnaissance Vautour, was taken while flying low over Bir Tamada. (AC)

Mission 101/6 departed Khatsor at 0800hrs, callsign LAMP, tasked to bomb again targets 1 and 2 along Beni Suef runway 01/19. The previous JORDAN and TIGRIS strikes had claimed the destruction of 16 Tu-16s, a claim that exceeded the AIR4 evaluation that 15 Tu-16s were based at Beni Suef on the morning of June 5. (Obviously, the AIR4 evaluation may have been inaccurate and/or the JORDAN and TIGRIS claim was exaggerated.) Either way, the plain fact was that LAMP could not see a single Tu-16 that was not destroyed, burning, or smoking. Beni Suef's bomber force had been practically wiped out by 0840hrs at the latest. Also at 0800hrs, Mission 117/4 departed Ramat David tasked to bomb targets 1 and 3 along Cairo West runway 10/28, where the Mirages strafed three Tu-16s and one MiG-21.

Mission 109/2 was tasked to attack targets 3 and 4 along Kabrit runway 18/36 with runway-piercing bombs. However, Mystère 15 was not serviceable, so POTASH departed Ekron at 0808hrs as a three-ship formation. After bombing, POTASH 2 reported that a MiG-17 was trailing the Mystères. It turned out to be two MiG-17s, so POTASH reported "there is prey over Kabrit". However, control either failed to hear the radio transmission or understand the message, so no Mirages were vectored to help, even though there was a Squadron 101 patrol over Sinai. Flying Mission 109/2 as POTASH 1, Assaf Ben Nun recalled:

A MiG-17 threatened us but our orders were to destroy on the ground as many aircraft as possible regardless of risks so at first we ignored the MiG. After the first strafing pass I engaged the MiG-17 while ordering the other pilots to press on with the strafing passes. The MiG-17 had an afterburner and was absolutely superior to the Mystère. Moreover, our external fuel tanks were in short supply so we were told to avoid dumping these tanks and I was foolish enough to fight that MiG-17 without jettisoning the external fuel tanks.

I could not disengage. The MiG zoomed skywards again and again. Each time he zoomed, I theoretically could disengage but the risk was that he might dive right after the other Mystères and maybe even shoot down a Mystère. The final act of the combat was when the MiG-17 zoomed upwards. I followed but obviously I could not keep pace with the MiG-17. I had to let go and dive but at exactly the same moment I noticed that the MiG-17 – though high above me – was also beginning to dive. I maneuvered my Mystère accordingly to create a situation with a slight chance, maybe 1-to-100, that the MiG-17's dive would place the Egyptian fighter right in front of me. I figured that if he would drop right over me, or right behind me, then he would open fire so I waited until I actually sensed his shadow. I still did not see him but I sensed he was there and I squeezed the trigger. A moment later the MiG-17 dived right into my burst of gun fire.

The MiG-17 was definitely hit, but a subsequent ejection or crash was not observed. The Mystères disengaged and, owing to low fuel state, returned to Ekron rather than to Ramat David. POTASH reported that the engagement lasted some three minutes, that the MiG-17 fought properly, and that three aircraft had been destroyed on the ground.

AIR1 Statistics did not list that MiG-17 as a kill. AIR4 concluded that the MiG-17 crashed – within IAF circles a confirmation of an air-to-air kill through obscure intelligence channels became known as an "AIR4 kill" credit – and Assaf Ben Nun was credited with the first of his eventual total of five kills.

Next was Mission 105/3, which took off from Khatsor at 0810hrs tasked to bomb targets 3 and 4 on Inchas runway 18/36. KNESSET claimed destruction of three MiG-21s. Also at 0810hrs, Mission 116/2 left Ekron to bomb targets 1 and 3 on Fayid runway 18/36. CASTRO claimed destruction of one MiG as well as strafing a P-30 radar, an AAA emplacement, and a water tower. While Squadron 116 reported that CASTRO claimed to have destroyed several MiG-21s and two Su-7s, intact targets were hard to find so the Mystères strafed air base installations during the third pass. Either way, Fayid had ceased to function.

Mission 113/4 departed Khatsor at 0815hrs as the fifth and final *Focus* first-wave formation tasked to raid Bir Gafgafa. ROBE attacked targets 1 and 2 along runway 15/33 as planned, but there were no more combat aircraft to strafe. ROBE 1 strafed an antiaircraft emplacement during the first strafing pass and an armored vehicle during the second. ROBE then diverted to nearby Jabbel Umm Margham and strafed the P-30 radar station on top of the mountain.

Also at 0815hrs, Mission 116/4 took off from Ekron to bomb targets 1 and 2 along Abu Sueir runway 09/27 with six light runway-piercing bombs. TRUMAN encountered four enemy aircraft – MiG-21s, Su-7s, or a mix – over Abu Sueir, while an Su-7 was seen to take off during the strike. TRUMAN 4 sensed a hit at the rear end of his Mystère, lost control, and was forced to eject. Upon hitting the ground, the TRUMAN 4 pilot saw an Su-7 or a MiG-21 flying over him, so it is highly likely that an Egyptian aircraft had shot him down. TRUMAN claimed destruction on the ground of one aircraft.

The seven formations that attacked from 0840hrs claimed up to only 12 aircraft destroyed on the ground, plus one MiG-17 in the air, at the cost of one Mystère. The first 40 *Focus* strike formations claimed up to 195 aircraft destroyed on the ground, plus eight aircraft in the air, for the loss of nine aircraft; a claims-to-loss ratio of 22.5-to-1 that could hardly have been achieved in any other scenario.

First wave completion

Five formations tasked to strike four EAF bases at 0855hrs and 0910hrs completed the *Focus* first wave. By then – from 0840 to 0855hrs – the second *Focus* BDA mission had departed, Squadron 147 dispatched three more Fouga formations to support IDF Command South in northeast Sinai, and Squadron 119's first readiness pair – FENCE – scrambled from Ekron at 0848hrs. SOFA of Squadron 101 was approaching the end of its patrol over Sinai when SOFA 2 spotted an Il-14 flying low west of Jabel Libni, took the lead, opened fire on it, and

The Il-14 that Squadron 101's SOFA 2 shot down near Jabel Libni at around 0900hrs on June 5, 1967, as photographed from an IAF Piper. (AC)

damaged it. The Il-14 landed straight ahead along desert dunes some 4 miles west of Jabel Libni. Antiaircraft fire – possibly from Jabel Libni – damaged SOFA 1 that trailed SOFA 2 at low altitude and slow speed in order to engage the Il-14, so the pair returned to Khatsor, with SOFA 1 landing at 0915hrs and SOFA 2 at 0918hrs.

Three formations were tasked to strike from 0855hrs, but Mission 105/7 departed late so only two formations attacked from 0855hrs and claimed destruction of at least six aircraft. Three *Focus* first-wave strike formations were yet to attack, but postwar AIR1 drew an artificial line that ended Operation *Focus* first wave at 0900hrs.

Focus first-wave destruction claims to 0900hrs				
EAF base	AIR4 prewar evaluation of present aircraft	Claims	AIR4 postwar assessment of destructions	IAF losses
El Arish	7 MiG-17s	up to 7	7 MiG-17s and 1 Antonov	none
Jabel Libni	2 MiG-15/17s[1]	up to 4	4 MiG-15/17s	none
Bir Gafgafa	14 MiG-21s	up to 17	10 MiG-21s, 4 Mi-6s, 1 helicopter, and 4 unidentified	2 Ouragans
Bir Tamada	14 MiG-17s	up to 16	10 MiG-17s, 2 Il-14s, 3 Mi-6s, and 1 Mi-4	none
Kabrit	29 MiG-15s and 22 MiG-17s	up to 33	24 MiG-15/17s and 1 Il-14	2 Super Mystères
Fayid	14 MiG-19s, 14 MiG-21s, and 16 Su-7s	up to 32	22 MiG-21s, 6 MiG-17s, 1 Su-7, 1 Antonov, and 1 transport	1 Ouragan, 1 Mystère
Abu Sueir	27 Il-28s and 19 MiG-21s	up to 20	12 Il-28s, 6 MiG-21s, and 1 MiG-17	1 Mystère
Inchas	32 MiG-21s	up to 22	19 MiG-21s and 5 MiG-17s	1 Super Mystère
Cairo West	22 MiG-15/17s, 15 MiG-21s, and 15 Tu-16s	up to 35	11 Tu-16s, 8 MiG-21s, 5 Il-28s, and 5 MiG-15/17s	none
Beni Suef	15 Tu-16s	up to 16	10 Tu-16s	none
Total	277[2]	up to 202	185, including at least 166 combat aircraft[3]	8[4]

Notes:
1 Possibly decoys
2 Nominal force; IAF evaluated EAF serviceability at 65 percent
3 Including destructions on the grounds but excluding claims in the air
4 Plus one Fouga lost in a radar station strike mission

The success of the *Focus* first wave was overwhelming. Reports yielded that all targets in the four closest EAF bases, as well as in the farthest EAF base, had been destroyed. Claims concerning Fayid, Kabrit, Abu Sueir, Inchas, and Cairo West surpassed 50 percent when compared with the prewar AIR4 evaluation of EAF deployment.

It was also during this timeframe that hostilities were disclosed in public for the first time when Radio Cairo announced at 0850hrs that Israeli aircraft had attacked Egyptian airfields. It was probably only then that Jordan and Syria understood that Israel had attacked Egypt. Ten minutes later, at 0900hrs, IAF monitoring indicated that Syrian MiG-21s had been scrambled to fly a defensive patrol. At the same time, the IDF ordered to inform Jordan, via the United Nations Jordan Israel Mixed Armistice Commission, that the EAF had been destroyed.

A brief pause

Postwar, the IAF officially ended the *Focus* first wave at 0900hrs, but on the day itself, two first-wave formations were tasked to strike from 0910hrs, while the 45th and final *Focus* first-wave strike formation – Mission 105/7 – actually attacked around 0920hrs owing to a delayed takeoff.

Meanwhile, from 0855 to 0920hrs, Squadron 147 dispatched a seventh Fouga formation to support IDF Command South in northeast Sinai; this was actually the first IAF formation to finish fast turnaround on June 5. SCIRPUS departed Khatserim at 0747hrs on Mission 147/1 to strike an Egyptian radar station in Sinai, returned to Khatesrim by 0825hrs, and after 39 minutes on the ground took off again at 0904hrs on Mission 147/11, tasked to attack Egyptian artillery in northeast Sinai.

Also from 0855 to 0920hrs, two more Mirage two-ship formations were scrambled to patrol, one over Galilee and one over Sinai. Meanwhile, Squadron 119's FENCE did not replace Squadron 101's SOFA to patrol over Sinai but was instead vectored to Abu Sueir, where EAF fighters had engaged all four *Focus* formations that attacked from 0810 to 0855hrs. FENCE flew to Abu Sueir at 25,000ft and arrived after 20 minutes. The pair circled over Abu Sueir for several minutes, while descending to 12,000ft and watching the 0910hrs strike. FENCE 1 saw a seemingly intact MiG-21 at the end of a taxiway, and planned to dive and strafe when that MiG-21 started to run along the taxiway. The MiG-21 departed, headed west, turned south, and climbed. FENCE 1 deployed its air brakes, launched a Shafrir air-to-air missile, which missed, then opened fire with its cannon, which also missed. The MiG-21 probably sensed FENCE 1's attack or had been warned and reversed its turn to the right. FENCE 1 followed, opened fire again and this time the MiG-21 exploded, entered a spin, and crashed. No ejection was seen.

FENCE returned to Abu Sueir, this time flying at 1,000ft, to look for more MiGs. FENCE 2 saw a MiG-21 and shot it down. Two more MiG-21s were then engaged, FENCE 2 shooting down one of them. FENCE 1 crossed the other MiG-21 head-on, and after several stitches – maneuvering in the vertical with afterburner on in order to preserve energy – managed to get into a hasty gunnery position, opened fire, missed, and disengaged. FENCE 2 – immediately after shooting down his

Mission 119/4 departed Ekron at 0845hrs to photograph Inchas, Abu Sueir, Fayid, and Kabrit with a low-altitude panoramic camera because all four bases were within the engagement envelope of Egyptian SA-2s. The Mission Order specified flying to targets at 100ft AGL but photographing from 500ft. This photograph was taken over Abu Sueir at around 0925hrs. (AC)

second MiG-21 – saw another MiG-21 flying alongside to his left. The MiG-21 turned away. FENCE 2 was unable to pursue owing to his low fuel state and had already switched off afterburner, so he turned after the MiG-21, fired, missed, and disengaged. AIR1 Statistics initially listed two kills for FENCE 2 and one for FENCE 1, but the tally was amended to three and one. AIR1 History apparently adhered to the credit of three kills. The IAF credited four kills split equally between FENCE 1 and 2.

At 0920hrs, the IAF reported to the IDF that 150 EAF aircraft had been destroyed, a cautious and conservative report. At the same time, IDF Intelligence informed the IDF that Egypt had ordered the Egyptian command of the Jordanian armed forces to begin artillery bombardment of IAF bases and to initiate battle procedure for nocturnal commando raids against IAF bases.[9]

Giora Romm – photographed postwar in the cockpit of the Squadron 119 Mirage that Eithan Carmi flew as FENCE 1 from 0848hrs on June 5, while Romm flew as FENCE 2 in another Mirage – became the first IAF ace. AIR1 Statistics initially credited Romm with four air-to-air kills during the Six-Day War, then AIR1 Statistics Amendment credited him with six, but it is believed that the IAF awarded Romm certificates crediting five kills. (ILGD/A)

Focus first-wave missions, sorties, air-to-air kills, and losses[1]							
Squadron	Patrol missions/ sorties	SEAB[2] missions/ sorties	Support missions/ sorties	Other missions/ sorties	Total	Kills[3]	Losses
101 Mirage	2/4	5/16	-/-	-/-	7/20	2	-
105 Super Mystère	-/-	9/34	-/-	-/-	9/34	3[4]	3
107 Ouragan	-/-	4/15	-/-	-/-	4/15	-	-
109 Mystère	-/-	4/15	-/-	-/-	4/15	1	1
110 Vautour	-/-	4/14	-/-	2/3[5]	6/17	-	-
113 Ouragan	-/-	8/33	-/-	-/-	8/33	1	3
116 Mystère	-/-	4/16	-/-	-/-	4/16	-	1
117 Mirage	2/4	4/16	-/-	1/2[6]	7/22	-	-
119 Mirage	1/2	3/12	-/-	1/1[7]	5/15	4	-
147 Fouga	-/-	-/-	7/28	4/16[8]	11/44	-	1
Total	5/10	45/171	7/28	8/22	65/231	11	9

Notes:

1 Departures from 0714 to 0919hrs.

2 Strike Enemy Air Bases missions that departed tasked to SEAB but not including missions that were retasked to SEAB.

3 IAF credited air-to-air kills; a credited kill was certified in a certificate awarded to the pilot.

4 Two observed ejections from MiG-21s over Abu Sueir are not included.

5 One jamming mission and one reconnaissance mission.

6 One escort mission.

7 One reconnaissance mission.

8 Four missions tasked to strike Egyptian radar stations in Sinai.

9   Egypt assumed supreme command of Jordan's armed forces in line with the Egyptian-Jordanian mutual defense treaty that was signed in Cairo on May 30, 1967, in order to tighten the ring around Israel; a short while later, an Egyptian commando force was deployed to Jordan.

Second wave

IAF operations obviously slowed down during transition from the first wave to the second; only eight combat aircraft sorties departed after 0855hrs, when the final first-wave strike formation departed, until 0933hrs, when the first *Focus* second-wave strike formation took off. The general guidelines for *Focus* second-wave strike formations were to finish their fast turnaround and then repeat the first-wave mission unless ordered otherwise. AIR3 actually managed to issue Mission Orders for *Focus* second-wave formations, which were distributed from headquarters directly to squadrons via a network of encrypted teleprinters. Additional information from headquarters or specific enquiries from squadrons were telephoned; an unsecured method, but relatively safe, and in any case the brief conversations touched upon specific subjects without exposure of the full mission order details. Still, from the *Focus* second wave onwards – when meticulous prewar planning no longer applied – there were quite a number of changes, mainly in missions' targets, mostly communicated prior to departure, but sometimes during ingress. This was primarily due to conflicting timings of strikes, as well as real-time analysis of the target's status – to what extent it had been destroyed and suppressed.

A minute after the first *Focus* second-wave strike formation departed – Mission 113/9 tasked to strike Fayid – the reconnaissance Vautour that flew Mission 110/5 returned to Ramat David at 0934hrs and the film was rushed off to process the BDA images of Bir Gafgafa and Bir Tamada. Ten *Focus* second-wave strike formations departed from 0934 to 0955hrs tasked to strike four EAF bases that had been attacked during the first wave – Bir Gafgafa, Abu Sueir, Fayid, and Kabrit – and three EAF bases that had not been attacked: Bilbeis, Mansura, and Minya. The reconnaissance Mirage that flew Mission 119/4 then returned to Ekron at 0958hrs to generate BDA images of EAF bases near the Suez Canal and beyond.

Additionally, from 0933 to 1010hrs, Squadron 147 dispatched three formations to support IDF Command South in northeast Sinai – one Fouga being lost to antiaircraft fire – and the Mirage squadrons scrambled two more pairs to patrol. Arab reaction to *Focus* was still verbal and local. At 0942hrs, Egypt announced that 23 Israeli aircraft had been shot down, and then at 1010hrs, that 42 had been destroyed, but more than two hours after H-Hour, Jordan and Syria still seem to have lacked information about what was really going on and had not yet reacted. By then, *Focus* had achieved its objective of air superiority and IAF combat aircraft could be tasked to support the IDF ground forces much sooner than expected.

A Squadron 119 reconnaissance Mirage photographing Inchas from low altitude, with at least three destroyed MiG-21s and one seemingly intact MiG-17 in the frame. The EAF dispersed dummy aircraft – some in unlikely positions for real combat aircraft to be parked – but did not disperse combat aircraft. In some cases an EAF aircraft hit during a strafing pass would ignite and destroy any neighboring aircraft parked too close; this appears likely here. (AC)

Ouragan pilots Dov Peleg, right, and Nachum Yahalom, left, in the Squadron 113 operations cell after their return from Mission 113/12. The IAF listed that *Focus* second-wave mission as an SEAB mission, but it was actually a support mission. Earlier, from 0745hrs, Peleg and Yahalom flew Mission 113/8 to strike Fayid. They flew in both as SHIRT 1 and SHIRT 3 respectively. Each flew one more mission during June 5, striking targets in Jordan. (AC)

The first IAF combat aircraft formation to fly a support mission was Squadron 107's SENECIO that departed Lod at 1010hrs on Mission 107/5, tasked to strike Egyptian artillery at Tart Umm Basis in support of IDF Command South's Division 38. The first Squadron 113 formation to fly a support mission was SHIRT, that departed Khatsor at 1018hrs to attack Egyptian artillery that engaged IDF Command South's Division 84 in northeast Sinai.

Ten formations departed from 1002 to 1101hrs tasked to strike EAF bases, including Helwan, which had not been attacked during the first wave. Parallel to the *Focus* second wave, from 1019 to 1055hrs, the IAF dispatched seven Squadron 147 Fouga formations to support the IDF; one Squadron 107 formation to strike an Egyptian radar station in Sinai; two Mirage pairs to patrol; and one pair of Mirages to photograph Inchas.

At 1102hrs, Radio Damascus announced that the SAF had been ordered to attack Israel, but there were still no actual signs of SAF – or JAF – offensive action. Three minutes later, at 1105hrs, the IDF noted that at least 180 Egyptian aircraft had been hit, again a very cautious evaluation, well below the number of pilots' claims, and a lot less than the actual destruction as shown in BDA photos. Still, the destruction of so many EAF aircraft signaled air superiority and the IDF issued, also at 1105hrs, guidelines for future IAF support. IDF Command South planned for Day 1 penetration through the front line and the initiation of a decisive armor battle in Sinai from the morning of Day 2. After supporting the IDF penetration, the IAF was tasked to strike and soften up Egyptian armor in Sinai in preparation for the planned clash with IDF Command South armor. The IAF's response, from receiving guidelines to implementing them, was so fast and flexible that TROUSER departed Khatsor at 1114hrs on Mission 113/14 tasked to strike the dreaded Division 4, an elite Egyptian armored division that had been deployed in the Bir Gafgafa sector.

Postwar, AIR1 History defined the Operation *Focus* second wave as lasting from 0934 to 1118hrs, a somewhat arbitrary delimitation that one might think referred to formations' departure times but was probably not so: AIR1 History listed 164 Operation *Focus* second-wave fighter force sorties, including 115 sorties in 35 formations tasked to strike EAF bases, but this text counts 120 fighter force sorties that departed at 0933–1118hrs, excluding the 38 support sorties by Squadron 147. It is therefore reasonable to assume that the AIR1 History definition of Operation *Focus*'s second wave lasted past 1118hrs departures, and this assumption is supported by the AIR1 History summary of the second-wave results:

- Destruction on the ground of 94 Egyptian aircraft out of 107 claims.
- Shooting down of four Egyptian aircraft and three Syrian aircraft.
- Loss of one Mirage.

The formations that had been credited with five of the aforementioned kills, as well as the formation that had lost a Mirage, departed after 1118hrs.

BANIAS to Luxor

AIR4 reported that a cell of Egyptian Tu-16 bombers that departed on a training mission that same morning, probably before *Focus* H-Hour, was diverted to land at Luxor. AIR3 issued Squadron 110 a mission order to strike Luxor, where the presence of four Tu-16s was expected,[10] and Squadron 110 assigned three Vautours to fly the mission to Luxor: BANIAS 1 and 2 with guns and BANIAS 3 with cameras but without guns. While BANIAS 3 was tasked to photograph Luxor, BANIAS 1 and 2 were tasked to strafe with more than enough firepower to destroy the expected cell of Tu-16s.

While planning this mission, Squadron 110 noted that the Vautours would be flying within 20km of Hurghada, an Egyptian fighter base that had not been attacked yet. The worried Vautour crews contacted AIR3 and were reassured that planning was under way to raid Hurghada before the Vautours would get there. Flying that mission as BANIAS 2, Herzle Bodinger (later to be IAF Commander from 1992 to 1996) recalled:

We were briefed to attack Luxor because Egyptian bombers had sought refuge in this distant air base that was supposedly beyond the limit of our radius of action. Many aircraft returned from the first wave with battle damage so only three Vautours could be assigned to fly the mission to Luxor. One of the three aircraft was a Vautour B that could only lift two 500kg bombs, rather than eight smaller bombs on quadruple bomb racks, due to center of gravity issues. The Vautour B was also tasked to take battle damage assessment images so each time we strafed, the Vautour B flew a photographic pass.

We flew an economical climb cruise along a straight line from Ramat David to Luxor. Hurghada was nearby that line. We were high so they could see us on their radar screens; all they had to do in order to thwart our mission was to scramble their Hurghada-based fighters to engage us. They need not even shoot us down; a few acts of air combat maneuvers and we would not be able to make it to Luxor, or if we would have been forced to jettison our bombs then we would no longer be able to press ahead to Luxor. We knew that Squadron 119 was tasked to attack Hurghada and to intercept enemy aircraft, if there would

10 Obviously, IAF AIR4 indicated that EAF bombers used to operate in three-aircraft cells so it would have been more probable for three or six Tu-16s to be expected at Luxor, but perhaps somewhere along the pipeline from AIR4 to AIR3 to Squadron 110 someone less knowledgeable interpreted an EAF bomber cell as a standard IAF strike formation of four aircraft.

All of the IAF Primary Training Squadron instructors, as photographed in February 1967, had an emergency posting back to the front-line squadron they flew with prior to joining the Flying School. To preserve their combat qualifications, they flew one day per week in their emergency posting squadrons and participated in a large-scale exercise after every four-month term. Standing (left to right) are: Oded Flum, Jeff Peer, Shmulik BenRom, Primary Training Squadron Commander Eliezer Prigat, Yochai Richter, Herzle Bodinger, Yair Sela, and Gabi Gerson; crouching (left to right) are: Zvika Rosenberg, Itamar Neuner, Ran Tsur, and Iftach Sadan (AC)

be any over Hurghada, so from the moment we saw Hurghada we watched and waited. Suddenly we saw explosions and we were relieved; Hurghada was attacked and we could pass through.

We descended and accomplished absolute surprise. At first, AAA did not open fire and when they did, after a long time, it was scattered and ineffective. The aircraft were dispersed all over the airfield so we flew our two bombing runs and started strafing. Each strafing pass we destroyed two aircraft with the Vautour B trailing behind us and photographing the progress of the destruction process.

After three strafing passes there were still targets to be attacked so [BANIAS 1] Shlomo Keren decided that we would continue until destruction of all targets. We flew six strafing passes and destroyed all targets. Keren's decision was correct but the additional passes consumed our fuel reserves. Just as we disengaged I was hit and soon afterwards I noticed that the port fuel gauge was dropping fast. There were two types of fuel gauges, total fuel and feeding fuel. Each engine had its own 400-liter [105-gallon] feeding fuel tank and the troublesome gauge was of the port feeding tank. I reported to my leader and he replied "You have a fuel leak, I can see." Using the cross-feed valve I tried to transfer fuel from the 'bad' side to the 'good' side but the starboard fuel gauge also began to drop; presumably the leak was from a critical point. I stopped crossover transfer and could only hope for the best. We were already cruising at 40,000ft and had already covered about half the distance [back to base] when the port engine flamed out. I could not maintain altitude on one engine so I slowly descended until steady state was accomplished at 25,000ft. The two Vautours escorted me and I began to think that I might reach Eilat [airfield]. There was a discussion whether I should try to land at Eilat – a short runway at the time – and I decided to try if I would ever get there.

The starboard engine flamed out as I flew over Eilat port and I glided to touch down exactly on the threshold of the runway. I was surprised that the landing run was so short and only then I realized that I had never landed a net weight Vautour without bombs and fuel. I opened the canopy, walked to the wingtip and prepared to jump but by the time I got there, hundreds of citizens surrounded the aircraft. I then saw the firemen climbing on their ladder to the empty cockpit and I had to force my way to warn them that the ejection seat had not been secured. I am not a big guy so they looked at me and asked "Who are you?" [I replied] "I am the pilot" and I could see that they were puzzled how such a small pilot flew such a big aircraft!

The excited Eilat citizens transported Bodinger to the City Mayor. AIR4 indicated that 15 aircraft had been destroyed at Luxor – five Tu-16s, eight Antonov transports, and two

Only Squadron 110's BANIAS was tasked to attack Luxor, a relatively large air base with 14 pens for large aircraft and two intersecting runways – 02/20 and 12/30 – which were long enough for bombers, with each having a parallel taxiway. In this photograph, the black smoke likely comes from two or three burning Tu-16s. An airlifter, possibly an Il-18, on the 12/30 taxiway has caught fire, while possibly an An-24 looks like it is taxiing into the pen. An An-12 can be seen on the 02/20 taxiway at the left. (AC)

airliners – while Squadron 110 reported that BANIAS claimed destruction of eight Tu-16s and eight An-12s. AIR1 History stated that BANIAS claimed destruction of 18 aircraft, including eight Tu-16s. BANIAS 2 reported destruction of three Tu-16s, two An-12s, and one C-54 Skymaster. Therefore, the actual claim was most likely the destruction of at least 12 aircraft, since the two strafing Vautours flew at least six passes each.

AIR1 History listed the Squadron 110 mission to Luxor as a *Focus* second-wave mission, even though takeoff was at 1125hrs and time on target was 1215hrs, both well after the 1118hrs arbitrary ending of the second wave. This book includes departures up to 1155hrs as part of the second wave, and thus regards the Luxor mission as part of that.

Jordan joins

Egypt initiated the crisis supposedly to protect Syria, while Jordan allied itself with Egypt and Syria as the crisis evolved. The first indication that Jordan joined hostilities surfaced at 1131hrs when the IDF was notified that Jordanian artillery had opened fire in the Jerusalem sector. The IDF permitted Command Center to return fire, but at 1140hrs Jordanian artillery started to bombard Ramat David, so at 1150hrs Israel's Defense Minister approved the IAF's request to task the IAF to attack Jordanian field artillery and strike Jordanian air bases. By then the aerial balance of forces in the Middle East was dramatically different than it had been only four hours earlier, but Jordan most likely had no realistic information at the time of the decision to attack Israel. Avihu Ben-Nun, Squadron 116 Deputy A in June 1967 and IAF Commander from 1987 to 1992, recalled:

> Years later I visited Jordan on a business trip and I was invited to dinner. One of the hosts who sat beside me said "I must tell you something. I was a ground controller at Karak in 1967. We saw all the aircraft that flew over Israel above 500 to 1,000ft. King Hussein called us on the morning of June 5, 1967, and said 'Nasser told me that there is a war and that the Egyptians are attacking Israel, that they are winning the war and that we should join hostilities. What do you see?' We saw nothing. Sometime later we saw aircraft emerging from Egyptian air bases and flying towards Israel. We figured that Nasser was truthful and King Hussein decided to join hostilities. Twenty minutes later we realized that something was wrong, the supposedly Egyptian aircraft did not return to their bases!" They actually saw our aircraft returning from the first wave missions, by the time they realized their error it was too late, King Hussein already ordered to open fire.

From 0933 to 1155hrs, the IAF had dispatched 32 formations tasked to strike 14 EAF bases. Eight formations were retasked during ingress. The first three retaskings were due to planning shortfalls, mostly overlapping times over target. The next five retaskings were in response to real-time analysis, mostly diversion of formations from targets that were reportedly suppressed to targets that were evaluated to be still operational. Egyptian AAA and SA-2 batteries were active, but EAF activity diminished and the strikers suffered no losses.

AIR1 History reported the claimed destruction on the ground of 204 aircraft during the first wave and 107 aircraft during the second wave. AIR4 indicated destruction on the ground of 187 or 189 aircraft during the first wave and 94 aircraft during the second wave. On top of destructions on the ground, IAF pilots were credited with four air-to-air kills during the second wave for a total of 13–15 Egyptian aircraft destroyed in the air during the first two waves.

Additionally, from 0933 to 1155hrs, the IAF dispatched 26 fighter force missions – 78 sorties – including 14 support, eight patrol, two tasked to strike radars, one electronic warfare, and one reconnaissance. The 14 support missions included ten Squadron 147 missions, during which one Fouga was lost, the one and only IAF loss during the *Focus* second wave. IAF losses were now up to ten, and the losses per sortie figure dropped to 2.3 percent.

Mirage gun camera photos reportedly taken while strafing Fayid; if so, this is the Squadron 117 second-wave mission. It is possible that the strafing Mirage fired two bursts during this pass, since in the first three frames, rounds are exploding but the Mirage is not firing – no black wedge in the corner – but it is firing in the next two, probably aiming at the third, farthest aircraft. The difficulty of pinpointing a target to strafe is evident. (AC)

Squadron	Patrol missions/ sorties	SEAB[2] missions/ sorties	Support missions/ sorties	Other missions/ sorties	Total	Kills[3]	Losses
Focus second-wave missions, sorties, air-to-air kills, and losses[1]							
101 Mirage	3/6	4/11	-/-	-/-	7/17	-	-
105 Super Mystère	-/-	7/26	-/-	-/-	7/26	-	-
107 Ouragan	-/-	1/4	2/6	1/4[4]	4/14	-	-
109 Mystère	-/-	4/16	-/-	-/-	4/16	1	-
110 Vautour	-/-	3/11	-/-	1/1[5]	4/12	-	-
113 Ouragan	-/-	4/13	3/12	1/3[6]	8/28	-	-
116 Mystère	-/-	3/12	-/-	-/-	3/12	-	-
117 Mirage	6/11	3/12	-/-	-/-	9/23	4	1
119 Mirage	3/6	3/12	-/-	1/2[7]	7/20[8]	3	-
147 Fouga	-/-	-/-	10/38	-/-	10/38	-	1
Total	12/23	32/117	15/56	4/10	63/206	8	2

Notes:
1 Departures from 0933 to 1214hrs
2 Strike Enemy Air Base missions that departed tasked to SEAB, but not including missions that were retasked to SEAB
3 IAF credited air-to-air kills; a credited kill was certified in a certificate awarded to the pilot
4 One mission to strike a radar station in Sinai
5 One mission to jam SA-2
6 One mission to strike a radar station in Sinai
7 One mission to photograph and strike Inchas
8 APARTMENT initiated two missions during this timeframe: one from 0935hrs and another from 1135hrs

OPPOSITE
Itamar Neuner graduated from the IAF Flying School Class 42 in November 1963. He first flew Ouragans, progressed to the Super Mystère in 1964, then the Mirage in 1965, and from 1966 served as a Flying School instructor with an emergency posting as a Squadron 119 Mirage pilot. He flew five sorties on June 5: Cairo West as LINTEL 4 from 0727hrs, Minya as LINTEL 4 from 0948hrs, scrambling as LINTEL 2 from 1234hrs, Cairo International as APARTMENT 4 from 1710hrs, and a scramble to patrol from 2202 to 2305hrs. (AC)

Third wave

Operation Order 67/11 _Focus_ did not specify an H-Hour for a second wave. The _Focus_ concept was of continuously launching missions as soon as aircraft were turned around. Therefore, other than H-Hour first wave it is difficult to define when a following _Focus_ wave started.

The first sign of a third wave surfaced earlier than the official 1155hrs starting point, at 1135hrs when Squadron 119's APARTMENT departed on a third mission to strike an enemy air base – but this book draws the line between the second and third waves at 1155hrs because after this point, the next formation to depart on a mission to strike an enemy air base would, eventually, attack an air base in Jordan.

The _Focus_ third wave mostly targeted Jordanian and Syrian air bases. IAF exploitation of air superiority had been suspended during this period after the two Ouragan squadrons were shifted from support to superiority.

Syria strikes

At 1150hrs the Israeli Defense Minister authorized the IDF to strike JAF bases, and at 1215hrs the IDF passed the order to the IAF. During this timeframe Syrian artillery opened fire and the IDF indicated at 1159hrs that Command North had been permitted to respond with counterbattery fire. At around that time the IAF detected SAF activity so, between 1154hrs and 1205hrs, Squadron 117 scrambled four pairs of Mirages to patrol over northern Israel. One Mirage malfunctioned and did not take off, leaving seven to patrol. From 1210hrs onwards, two formations engaged enemy aircraft over northern Israel. The formation that departed at 1154hrs

(therefore *Focus* second wave) engaged at around 1210hrs and again at around 1215hrs, and was credited with two kills. The formation that departed at 1205hrs engaged enemy aircraft at around 1220hrs, and was credited with one kill for the loss of one Mirage (part of the third wave).

At around that time Hunters appeared over the Command Center theater of operations. Those Hunters were probably both Iraqi and Jordanian. It is most likely that the Iraqi Hunters operated opposite Samaria and the JAF Hunters opposite Judea, a division between Iraqi and Jordanian armed forces that had been first fielded back in 1948. Four of the Hunters attacked Sirkin airfield at around 1221hrs. Sirkin airfield – formerly RAF Petah Tikva, the home of the IAF Flying School until 1955 and from that time onwards the base of the IDF Officers' School – was not a fully active IAF air base, but a few Dakota and Nord transports had been deployed there in order to disperse IAF assets and relieve congestion at IAF main bases. The Hunters destroyed a Nord; they were most likely Iraqi, because no Jordanian narrative concerning such a strike ever surfaced, and Sirkin was in the traditional Iraqi theater of operations. At that time IAF Mirage patrols flew over northern Israel to engage the SAF, so the low-flying Hunters were not detected and were not engaged over Israel. At 1234hrs, Squadron 119's LINTEL was scrambled. Flying as LINTEL 2, in his personal wartime log Itamar Neuner wrote:

The Squadron 103 Nord destroyed at Sirkin airfield was the only aircraft that IAF lost on the ground on June 5, 1967. (AC)

> My third sortie was [a] scramble – with [Oded] Sagee – to patrol, at 5,000ft, between Ramla and Sirkin, looking for Jordanian Hunters that had attacked Sirkin and set a Nord on fire. Control repeatedly asked us to look around but we saw nothing unusual. After a while we were vectored to Mafraq airfield in Jordan.
>
> The radio was saturated – it later transpired that all the Nords [that were scrambled from Ekron] were chattering over the emergency channel – so communication was broken but in the end we received a report that two Hunters were at our three o'clock... Sagee saw them and descended towards them. I trailed behind him... saw a Hunter far away in the west, jettisoned fuel tanks and accelerated to Mach 1.1 at an altitude

below 10,000ft. They [the two Hunters] did a coordinated turn inside. At first I followed the Hunter that turned south but I then switched to the Hunter that turned north. While I was right behind the Hunter – range 600m and fast overtake speed – he jettisoned the fuel tanks and I had to break away to avoid a collision with the tanks. He also turned left. I did not want to enter scissors so I pulled up and he followed me so I descended and disengaged. The other Hunter then followed me and Sagee directed me as a bait while he was getting organized to open fire which he did after a while. He hit the Hunter in its wing and I saw the ejection of the pilot.

Attacking the JAF and SAF

Radio Cairo announced at 1240hrs that 70 Israeli aircraft had been destroyed – a 700 percent over-claim – at a time when the IAF concluded that the EAF had been practically destroyed and air superiority accomplished. The IAF therefore decided to stop striking EAF bases and, in line with IDF guidelines, start striking JAF bases and SAF bases. Referring to the situation at around that time, IAF Commander Moti Hod recalled:

I knew… that no other air force in the Middle East, except for [the] EAF, could inflict serious damage upon us and indeed they did not… Actually, from noon, most of [the] IAF was committed to interdiction. We stopped attacking [Egyptian] air bases at 1200hrs… with all Ouragans and all Fougas and all Mystères already available [for support]. As a matter of fact, from 0900hrs I had nothing to do with them. We finished the four airfields in Sinai that had been attacked by Super Mystères, Mystères and Ouragans so that from then on I could do nothing with these aircraft because deep interdiction was beyond their range. They all stood and waited…

Squadron 107 pilot Amnon Gurion departed Lod in Ouragan 80 at 1401hrs as SENECIO 2 to strike Amman. Ouragan 80 was unique among the IAF fighter force at that time as the only aircraft to wear a lighter camouflage scheme, which would become an IAF standard scheme after the Six Day War. The outfit of the maintainers indicates that they are reservists. (BIAF)

Squadron 105's Super Mystère 34 flew Mission 105/20 from 1304hrs as DUBEK 1 and was photographed in July 1967 adorned with a kill marking under the windshield. Super Mystère 34 flew five sorties on June 5: striking Inchas from 0758hrs, Abu Sueir from 1004hrs, Saikal from 1304hrs, and Inchas from 1636hrs, and supporting Command Center from 2113hrs. (AC)

It was not decided in advance. When to stop attacking air bases? When to switch from Egypt to Syria and Jordan? These were all decisions that I made… I decided at 1200hrs to stop attacking Egyptian air bases and to proceed to the phase of air combats.

At around 1245hrs, two formations flying to strike EAF bases were ordered to turn back and attack Jordan. Departing Ekron at 1215hrs, Squadron 119's FLOOR, tasked to strike Hurghada after APARTMENT, was retasked to strike Amman; Squadron 105's NOBLESSE departed Khatsor at 1221hrs tasked to strike Mansura, but was retasked during ingress to attack Inchas and then retasked again to strike the Jordanian radar station at Ajloun.

From 1246 to 1410hrs, the IAF dispatched 22 formations to strike two JAF bases – Amman and Mafraq – and four SAF bases: Baly, Dumayr, Mazzeh, and Saikal. Those 22 formations comprised 24 Super Mystères in six formations, eight Vautours in two formations, 23 Mystères in six formations, and 31 Ouragans in eight formations. During this period, Mirages were not tasked to strike enemy air bases but flew patrols, while (contrary to some memoirs and recollections) Ouragans and Mystères continued to strike the air bases.

Two major factors had changed by the time the IAF attacked the Syrian and Jordanian air bases: relative strength and tactical surprise. Having destroyed the EAF, the IAF had become the largest air force in the Middle East – at least for the duration of hostilities – and was almost ten times more powerful than the JAF and nearly twice the combat aircraft strength of the SAF. On the other hand, tactical surprise was no longer realistic, and those two air forces

could be expected to fight back and inflict heavier losses upon IAF strikers than the Egyptians had.

The kill-to-loss ratio was therefore somewhat less dramatic than that of the first wave. Within an hour or so the IAF claimed roughly 40 percent of the SAF's inventory of combat aircraft destroyed on the ground, plus 80 percent of JAF Hunters, at the cost of one Vautour, three Mystères, and two Ouragans. As could be expected by then, almost exactly five hours after *Focus* H-Hour, JAF Hunters and SAF MiG-21s flew patrols to defend their air bases. JAF Hunters engaged IAF Mystères tasked to raid Mafraq, and SAF MiG-21s intercepted IAF Vautours and Super Mystères tasked to strike Dumayr and Saikal, respectively. Consequent combat over Jordan resulted in a loss of a Mystère to a Hunter versus an IAF credit of a Hunter kill to a Mystère pilot. Ensuing engagements over Syria resulted in a loss of a Vautour to a MiG-21, while the IAF credited two MiG-21 kills, one each to a Super Mystère pilot. At the time flying Mission 105/20 to strike Saikal as DUBEK 2, Jeremy Keidar recalled:

We bombed as planned but when I rolled over at the top of the pull-up, I saw a MiG-21 head[-]on. Yalo[11] started turning to enable his wingman and the second pair to regroup with him, then to return for a strafing pass at the end of the 270-degree turn. Yalo turned, I followed and he probably looked back over his shoulder and started to count: 2, 3, 4[;] and another aircraft, a MiG-21, trailed Zohar![12]

Squadron 105's Super Mystère 65 flew Mission 105/20 from 1304hrs on June 5 as DUBEK 2 and was photographed in July 1967 adorned with a kill marking under the windshield. Super Mystère 65 flew five sorties on June 5: striking Inchas from 0740hrs, Abu Sueir from 1004hrs, and Saikal from 1304hrs, and supporting Command Center from 1822hrs and 2026hrs. (AC)

We were not surprised[13] and Yalo instructed Zohar over the radio how to evade the MiG-21. We were still flying low so we jettisoned the external fuel tanks and Yalo ordered Shokhat to disengage, climb to a higher altitude, fly without afterburner and wait for us.[14]

Yalo engaged the MiG that followed Zohar. The MiG was in a sandwich with Yalo trailing the MiG and instructing Zohar how to maneuver so that Yalo would accomplish an air-to-air kill position behind the MiG-21.

Then I saw a second MiG and I suppose that this was the MiG-21 that I encountered

11 Aaron Shavit – at the time Squadron 105 Commander – who flew Mission 105/20 as DUBEK 1.

12 Eli Zohar flying Mission 105/20 as DUBEK 4.

13 DAPHNE, the formation flying Mission 105/18 to strike Saikal ahead of Mission 105/20, had encountered MiG-21s, evaded combat, and reported to DUBEK that MiG-21s were in the air to defend Saikal.

14 Flying Mission 105/20 as DUBEK 3, during ingress antiaircraft fire hit his Super Mystère that pressed ahead with the mission but leaked fuel from the port external fuel tank; hence DUBEK 1 gave orders to DUBEK 3 so that DUBEK 3 would not activate afterburner on the one hand and would not return alone on the other.

head-on during the bombing run as there was not enough time for him to follow Zohar after crossing me. I engaged that MiG and we flew tight scissors. We were slow and well below 10,000ft; I reckon that we sunk 2,000ft per one act of scissors. During one of the crossovers we were really close, I saw his cockpit and he was not wearing a white helmet but a brown leather hat; at least that was my impression perhaps because of the color. Until then he flew and fought very well, much like us during training air-to-air combat sessions but during that specific close crossover he reversed too early. That was when I started to get the upper hand.

I rushed with my first cannon burst, [but] deflection angle was still too high and I missed. In the Super Mystère we had to switch the gyro sight to air-to-air mode and I noticed that the sight functioned only in pitch but not in yaw. I was too inexperienced and excited to try and fix the problem so I decided to open fire from so close that I just could not miss, what we called a "death burst": a long burst from very short range that was sprayed while pedaling with the legs. But my second cannon burst also missed.

All that time I heard Yalo over the radio. He instructed Zohar who was in a delicate situation as the MiG was right behind him and firing. According to Yalo they finished the engagement on the deck, really low. All that time I was all alone. When Yalo did not talk over the radio, Shokhat did; he flew high above, had a grand view of the air combat and offered his advice.

Right after my second burst Yalo finally shot down the MiG-21 that threatened Zohar so he yelled over the radio: "DUBEK, all head west!" The rationale was to disengage from Saikal at first and then to regroup. I immediately replied "1, there is a MiG in front of me" and I really meant to report that I was about to shoot down a MiG so I cannot disengage immediately but Yalo – who did not hear me over the radio until then because they were all busy and I did not want to interfere with the rescue of Zohar – interpreted my message as "hey, what shall I do now?" So ever since, Yalo's story – and it is a great story – is that I asked him what to do, he replied "shoot him down" and I reported "I shot him down!"

I was in a dilemma. On the one hand the leader – acting as god in such a mission and if your leader was the squadron commander then he was even more than god – ordered to disengage. On the other hand I was fighting a MiG-21 and I had the upper hand. I already fired twice and missed but by then my position was much better. How could I disengage? I closed the distance to well below 200 meters for the death burst and exactly at this moment I heard Yalo over the radio [saying] "so shoot him down!" I squeezed the trigger and the rounds ripped off a wing. The MiG spun in and immediately crashed. We were flying low, so I reported, "I shot him down" and I disengaged.

DAPHNE 1 indicated in the Mission 105/18 debrief that one MiG-21 had been destroyed on the ground and that DUBEK 1 shot down a MiG-21 near Saikal. The Mission 105/20 debrief stated:

All four [Super Mystères] attacked aiming point 1 [and] it seems that six bombs hit [the target]... Number 1 destroyed a MiG-21 [on the ground] at the end of [runway] 06. Two MiG-21s crossed us head-on during exit after bombing so we stopped strafing, engaged, jettisoned external fuel tanks at very low altitude. Number 2 hit the wing of one MiG, the wingtip disintegrated. Number 1 shot down the second MiG,

Squadron 105's DUBEK formation after returning from Mission 105/20 to strike Saikal, sometime after landing at 1405hrs and 1406hrs. From left to right are Squadron 105 Commander Aaron Shavit (known as Yalo), his wingman Jeremy Keidar, and DUBEK 4 Eli Zohar. (AC)

Ouragan 96 departed Khatsor at 1410hrs to fly Mission 113/21 to strike Mafraq as HAT 1. Antiaircraft fire hit the Ouragan, and Squadron 113 Commander Joseph Salant was forced to eject over the Mediterranean at around 1500hrs. Ouragan 87 returned to Khatsor from Mission 113/4 at 0916hrs and did not fly again until June 9, so we can deduce that this photo was taken between 0916 and 1410hrs. (ARC)

the pilot ejected and was killed… No activity was observed in the airfield… No antiaircraft fire over airfield.

Syrian antiaircraft fire was usually intense and fierce, so it is possible that the AAA emplacements defending Saikal were ordered to hold fire while Syrian MiG-21s engaged Israeli Super Mystères over the air base. AIR1 Statistics listed Shavit's kill but not Keidar's. However, AIR1 Statistics Amendment credited Shavit and Keidar with one kill per pilot.

The line between the *Focus* third wave and fourth wave is drawn, in this text, at 1415hrs departure time. Conceptually, *Focus* projected continuous operations so the division between waves is arbitrary and there was an overlap between waves: third-wave formations that departed closer to 1410hrs obviously attacked after 1415hrs; Squadron 113's HAT flew Mission 113/21 to strike Mafraq, departed Khatsor at 1410hrs, and returned by 1511hrs.

Still, IAF combat aircraft formations that departed up to 1410hrs are attributed to the *Focus* third wave, while departures from 1415hrs onwards are attributed to the fourth wave.

Focus third-wave missions, sorties, air-to-air kills, and losses[1]							
Squadron	Patrol missions/ sorties	SEAB[2] missions/ sorties	Support missions/ sorties	Other missions/ sorties	Total	Kills[3]	Losses
101 Mirage	3/6	1/4	-/-	-/-	4/10	-	1
105 Super Mystère	-/-	7/27	-/-	-/-	7/27	2	-
107 Ouragan	-/-	3/12	-/-	-/-	3/12	-	-
109 Mystère	-/-	3/11	-/-	-/-	3/11	-	1
110 Vautour	-/-	2/8	-/-	-/-	2/8	-	1
113 Ouragan	-/-	4/15	1/4[4]	-/-	5/19	-	2
116 Mystère	-/-	3/12	-/-	-/-	3/12	1	2
117 Mirage	6/12	-/-	-/-	-/-	6/12	1	-
119 Mirage	3/6	1/4	-/-	-/-	4/10	1	-
147 Fouga	-/-	-/-	9/31	-/-	9/31	-	1
Total	12/24	24/93	10/35	-/-	46/152	5	8

Notes:
1 Departures from 1215 to 1410hrs
2 Strike Enemy Air Base missions that departed tasked to SEAB but not including missions that were retasked to SEAB
3 IAF credited air-to-air kills; a credited kill was certified in a certificate awarded to the pilot
4 One mission to support Command South but tasked in the air to strike Mazzeh

Fourth wave

By the time *Focus* had progressed from the third to the fourth wave, losses of EAF combat aircraft had reached approximately 75 percent of the prewar order of battle; the JAF had been practically destroyed and the SAF combat aircraft inventory had been approximately halved. The Israelis had lost 16 combat aircraft – two Mirages, three Super Mystères, one Vautour, five Mystères, and five Ouragans – so the actual ratio of losses was approximately one IAF combat aircraft to 15 EAF/JAF/SAF combat aircraft, at a very conservative evaluation of 240 EAF/JAF/SAF combat aircraft destroyed in the air and on the ground during the first three waves.

Vautours strike Iraq's H-3 airfield

Iraqi Hunters had been attacking Israeli objectives in the sector opposite Samaria since around 1220hrs. The most successful strike was the aforementioned raid against Sirkin where an IAF Nord was destroyed on the ground and the aircraft's sentry killed. However, additional air strikes in the area from Sirkin in the south to Ramat David in the north were reported:

- At 1225hrs Command Center reported that enemy aircraft had attacked Nathanya.
- At 1305hrs Command North reported that enemy aircraft strafed a Brigade 5 mortar battery near Yavetz (these may have been the aircraft that raided Nathanya strafing a target of opportunity during egress, since Yavetz is roughly 10km east of Nathanya, and the presented times are the times of reports, not those of the attacks).
- At 1340hrs Command Center reported that three "Jordanian" aircraft were spotted flying west near Magal, but the location of Magal suggests that these were more likely Iraqi aircraft.
- At 1345hrs Command North clarified the picture with a report that at 1220hrs two enemy aircraft attacked an aluminum factory near Kfar Saba, where several workers were killed, while at 1230hrs six enemy aircraft were observed in the Tsufit to Sgula area and civilian casualties were reported at Nathanya, where a resident area had been attacked, as well as at Raanana, where a workshop had been hit.
- At 1350hrs Command Center reported that enemy aircraft raided Kfar Saba, Sgula Junction, Sirkin, Bakhan, Ramat HaKovesh, Nathanya, Raanana again, and Shaar Ephraim.

Only three Mirage formations attacked Jordanian air bases: Squadron 119's FLOOR that departed at 1215hrs, Squadron 101's ARMCHAIR that departed at 1341hrs, and Squadron 117's ALLEGRA that departed at 1426hrs. The Squadron 117 and Squadron 119 missions were four-ship formations tasked to strike Amman, while the Squadron 101 mission was a two-ship formation to protect the strike aircraft. This scene was most likely captured through the sight of an ARMCHAIR Mirage that strafed Amman at around 1415hrs. (AC)

All – except Sirkin airfield – are cities and villages opposite Samaria in the traditional Iraqi theater of operations.

At the time of the raids, the IAF and IDF assumed that the attacking Hunters were Jordanian. It was only at 1250hrs that Israel intercepted an Egyptian message to Iraq that was essentially a request to launch Iraqi air operations against Israel. If Iraqi Hunters indeed attacked Sirkin and other targets in Israel from around 1220hrs, then Iraq had already joined hostilities, but for Israel, at the time, the first indication of a probable Iraqi intervention was this intercepted message.

Many Mirages were in the air during this timeframe, but the Hunters that operated over the sector opposite Samaria escaped interception by flying low, below the detection envelope of IAF radar stations. This confirmed the IAF prewar assumption that Arab radar stations of equivalent technology were unable to detect low-flying aircraft, an assumption that was one of the building blocks of the *Focus* concept and made it unnecessary to attack enemy radar stations in advance of striking enemy air bases. Therefore, the most practical path for the IAF to disrupt or to end Iraqi air strikes was to raid the only Iraqi airfield within range and to destroy the Iraqi Hunters on the ground. AIR3 issued Mission 110/15, and four Squadron 110 Vautours departed Ramat David at 1415hrs to strike H-3. At the time flying as VISTULA 1, Gideon Magen recalled:

> The Fighting Executive asked me "do you know where H-3 is?" and I retorted "no, maybe in Jordan?" but he said "no, it is in Syria"… Our only intelligence information was that H-3 was a NATO patterned airfield with one runway and a parallel taxiway, a 1:500,000 scale map and coordinates.

A low mission profile – in and out, all the way – was planned because the SAF was not completely wiped out. Owing to the poor quality of the maps, the route was in a straight line from the southernmost point of the Sea of Galilee, heading almost exactly east for

The Squadron 110 Vautour pilots who flew the mission to strike H-3, photographed at the end of the war. From left to right are reserve pilot Ran Goren, who flew as VISTULA 3, reserve pilot Gideon Magen (VISTULA 1), and emergency posting pilot Jacob Tal (VISTULA 4). Magen, Goren, and Tal flew three sorties each on June 5. (AC)

some 28 minutes until rendezvous with a desert road, leading to H-3 after some two more minutes of flying.

Immediately after departure, VISTULA 2 reported a landing gear malfunction; the front wheel doors did not close. VISTULA 1 ordered his wingman to return to base and VISTULA pressed ahead as a three-ship formation. Gideon Magen recollected:

We rendezvoused with the road and pulled up on time. We did not identify the target when [VISTULA 4, Jacob] Tal reported "bogey, six o'clock". A break to the right and I saw them, two MiG-21s right behind [VISTULA 3 Ran] Goren and Tal. I ordered to keep looking for the target, followed the higher MiG and opened fire from a range of 800 yards; short burst, no hits. The lower MiG was in front of Tal; Tal opened fire, also from long range and also without apparent results, but he was in a sandwich with the other MiG behind him. I tried to warn him but my external communication system ceased to function as a result of the cannon burst; only the intercom still functioned.

Ran Goren then warned Tal and Tal broke away. The inconclusive engagement continued for four or five minutes while the Vautours flew east, looking for H-3. When VISTULA 1 finally spotted the Iraqi air base, he was unable to report to the wingmen owing to the failure of the communication system. Magen pulled up to bomb the target; he planned one bombing run from west to east – because he was flying a Vautour IIN with less fuel – and hoped that Goren and Tal would follow. While pulling up, Magen saw two Hunters and a MiG-21 taxiing to depart, so he changed his aiming, dropped all eight bombs on the nearest quarter runway point, thus preventing the departure of these aircraft and probably saving the day as the Hunters were unable to depart and intercept the Vautours. While VISTULA 1 was pulling up from dive bombing, Magen noted a line of four or five aircraft midway along the taxiway. Magen kept flying east to enable the pair, hopefully right behind him, enough space and time to bomb, turned 180 degrees and returned for a first strafing pass, aiming at the line that he had spotted during bombing. At the time flying as VISTULA 3, Goren recalled:

Communication with Magen ceased after he opened fire. Because of the intensive evasive maneuvers the pair I was leading separated so each aircraft flew independently. I could communicate with Tal but not with Magen. Suddenly we saw H-3, an airfield full of aircraft: silver MiGs, green Hunters and a large aircraft at the western end of the taxiway. I turned right to bomb from east to west, as planned, but because of the threat from MiG [aircraft in the air] I decided to cut the long climb for the bombing dive position and to strafe first. I turned left and dived northwards, perpendicular to the runway towards the large aircraft that looked like a Tu-16; a burst of cannon fire and that aircraft caught fire.

While Goren improvised that strafing pass, flying roughly from south to north, Tal improvised a bombing run along the single runway, generally flying from west to east, and Magen returned to strafe, generally flying from east to west and aiming at the line of aircraft along the taxiway. VISTULA 4's cluster of four bombs hit the runway. VISTULA 1 set on fire all aircraft at that line and also managed to strafe two aircraft parked in the western line. One of these caught fire before VISTULA 1 squeezed the trigger; it was the large aircraft – probably not a Tu-16 – that VISTULA 3 strafed. Then a shadow of an aircraft, VISTULA 3, flashed by underneath VISTULA 1. Goren remembered:

Exactly at that moment Tal ordered me to break. He bombed from west to east and saw that a MiG launched an air-to-air missile. I broke, the missile missed and the MiG flashed on my right and zoomed upwards. I turned left and planned to bomb perpendicular to the runway but then I saw the two MiGs flying higher and Tal reported that none was following me so

I changed my plan to bomb along the runway's axis from east to west. I saw two Hunters preparing for departure on the western end of the runway so I aimed to a point right in front of them, to block their departure.

VISTULA 3 also dropped all eight bombs in a single salvo. VISTULA 1 flew a second strafing pass, aiming at two parked Hunters in the face of ineffective antiaircraft fire – the two MiG-21s may have been waiting for the Vautours' attack to end in order to resume the engagement – finished the cannon ammunition, noted that fuel state was low, and decided to disengage. Goren recalled:

I turned left 270 degrees and strafed the two Hunters that were still holding in departure position. I flew a strafing pass from south to north and set them both on fire. Then I turned left and headed back home. Another Vautour also flew west. I assumed that this was Tal's aircraft and I ordered him to regroup with me; low altitude, 450 knots. Then I saw the third Vautour flying north of us; a brief discussion over the radio and I realized that I was flying alongside Magen – who was unable to communicate – with Tal north of us. Tal regrouped with us and then I noticed a MiG-21, flying a kilometer or so right behind Magen. I ordered Magen to break but he did nothing, [as] he could not hear me. I turned towards him and then I saw a trail of fire in pursuit of Magen, [but] the missile hit the ground some 50 meters behind the Vautour; it was a miracle.

VISTULA flew west with Magen in the middle, Tal to his right, and Goren on his left. At this point, two MiG-21s closed behind VISTULA 1 and VISTULA 3. Goren saw the MiG-21 behind Magen but did not see that behind his Vautour IIA, while Magen saw the MiG-21 behind Goren but did not see the one that followed his Vautour IIN. They were unable to warn each other because of the communication failure of VISTULA 1. Magen recalled:

Squadron 117's Mirage 45 as photographed in December 1967 during IDF Chief of Staff Isaac Rabin visit to Ramat David. The IAF credited Squadron 117 pilot Uri EvenNir with a Lebanese Air Force Hunter kill while flying Mirage 45 on June 5. The two Iraqi Air Force kill markings refer to Hunter and MiG-21 kills credited to Squadron 117 pilot Yehuda Koren in the wake of a mission to H-3 on June 6. (AC)

Shortly after we regrouped, we saw a MiG-21 approaching Goren. Initially the MiG flew some three kilometers behind Goren. We were unable to warn him so I turned towards him and then I saw a missile exploding on the ground behind his Vautour. [The MiG-21s disengaged] and I turned back and headed west again. Tal was no longer where we expected him to be and we saw an explosion. We feared the worst but then we saw him trailing behind us. Apparently, he dropped excessive bombs and this was the explosion that we saw.

VISTULA 1 reported a total claim of nine to 12 destroyed aircraft, while VISTULA 3 reported a total claim of six MiG-21s, five Hunters, and one large transport aircraft. AIR1 History reported claimed destruction of ten aircraft: six MiG-21s, three Hunters, and one transport aircraft.

No more enemy air strikes in the sector opposite Samaria were reported after VISTULA raided H-3 from around 1450hrs so, with VISTULA mission accomplished, AIR3 did not issue additional mission orders to strike H-3 within the timeframe of *Focus*.

Slowdown: 1415–1600hrs

One more air strike subsequently attributed to Iraqi Hunters took place after the departure of VISTULA and prior to their attack on H-3. Sometime between 1422hrs and 1430hrs, hostile Hunters appeared over Ramat David. The Hunters may have failed to pinpoint the camouflaged airfield or missed and attacked agricultural facilities around the adjacent village of Nahalal. The Israelis did not know if the hostile Hunters were Iraqi, Jordanian, or Lebanese. Two Mirage pairs were scrambled from Ramat David in the wake of the Hunters' overflight. One of those pairs intercepted a Lebanese Hunter over Rayaq and shot it down.

IAF activity slowed down between 1415hrs and 1600hrs. The *Focus* objectives had already been accomplished so demand for offensive air superiority missions declined. Mirages patrolled to defend against any counter-air offensive, but the EAF proved unable to counterattack and the Iraqi, JAF, and SAF strikes had been mostly negligible in impact and practically contained. In the Command South theater of operations, Squadron 147 continued to fly support missions, but demand for support was still limited so only two such combat missions were flown. Overall, the IAF dispatched 21 combat aircraft missions – encompassing 61 sorties – from 1415 to 1600hrs.

Focus fourth-wave missions, sorties, air-to-air kills, and losses[1]							
Squadron	Patrol missions/ sorties	SEAB[2] missions/ sorties	Support missions/ sorties	Other missions/ sorties	Total	Kills[3]	Losses
101 Mirage	3/6	1/3	-/-	-/-	4/9	-	-
105 Super Mystère	-/-	1/4	-/-	-/-	1/4	-	1
107 Ouragan	-/-	-/-	2/7	-/-	2/7	-	-
109 Mystère	-/-	1/3	-/-	-/-	1/3	-	-
110 Vautour	-/-	1/4	-/-	-/-	1/4	-	-
113 Ouragan	-/-	-/-	-/-	-/-	-/-	-	-
116 Mystère	-/-	2/7	-/-	-/-	2/7	-	-
117 Mirage	6/12	1/4	-/-	-/-	7/16	2	2
119 Mirage	1/2	2/7	-/-	-/-	3/9	2	-
147 Fouga	-/-	-/-	7/28	-/-	7/28	-	-
Total	10/20	9/32	9/35	-/-	28/87	4	3

Notes:
1 Departures from 1415 to 1554hrs
2 Strike Enemy Air Bases missions that departed tasked to SEAB but not including missions that were retasked to SEAB
3 IAF credited air-to-air kills; a credited kill was certified in a certificate awarded to the pilot

Mirages flew only two SEAB missions during the third wave but stepped up SEAB with five missions during the fourth wave, including two Squadron 119 missions tasked to strike T-4 in Syria. This Mirage gunsight photo was reportedly taken while strafing T-4, with the Mirage firing at what looks like a MiG-15UTI while flying over a tarpaulin-covered MiG-21. Only APARTMENT and LINTEL struck T-4. AIR4 reported five MiG-21s, three MiG-17s, and one Il-14 destroyed on the ground, while Giora Romm and Asher Snir shot down one MiG-21 each. (AC)

Fifth wave: 1600hrs until end of the day

The slowdown during the fourth wave was exploited to evaluate the situation. At around 1600hrs the IAF was ordered to stop strafing during air base attack missions, since the primary objective of strafing was to destroy enemy combat aircraft on the ground but most enemy combat aircraft had been destroyed and the balance was most likely dispersed or hidden inside hangars. The risk of being hit by enemy antiaircraft fire therefore outbalanced the probability of successfully destroying enemy combat aircraft on the ground. It became much more crucial to preserve the freshly won new balance of air power – IAF versus EAF, Iraqi, JAF, and SAF – than to destroy on the ground a few more enemy aircraft.

Also at around that time, the Ramat David Wing 1 Commander reportedly gathered all aircrews under his command, except for those on duty at the time, to present the situation and to stress that while the top priority that day had been to attack regardless of safety, from this point onwards the priority would be to preserve the IAF order of battle.

The IAF stopped attacking Egyptian air bases at around 1300hrs, yet the EAF did not launch offensive operations until sunset of Day 1, June 5. The fifth and final *Focus* wave was therefore mostly a limited lights-out effort aimed at striking selected Egyptian air bases in order to disrupt the repair of battle damage during the night.

Exploitation of air superiority had not been expected to start before Day 2, but the IAF supported Command South throughout *Focus*, using Fouga armed trainers of Squadron 147 while combat aircraft – Ouragans – flew support missions during the *Focus* second and fourth waves.

At 1600hrs, AIR3 issued Operation Order 67/68 NACHSHONS 80. The objective of Operation *Nachshons 80* was to support IDF Command South's Division 38 offensive against the Egyptian Umm Qattef fortifications through a Brigade 80 attack against the rear of the fortifications. The IAF allocation to Operation *Nachshons 80* included 15 Nords and one Stratocruiser fixed-wing transport, along with 18 Sikorsky S-58s and three or four Super Frelons helicopters. The transports were tasked to drop a Brigade 80 battalion from 1935hrs or 1945hrs. The helicopters were tasked to insert the bulk of Brigade 80 in an air train from 1900hrs. Obviously, an airlift in the combat zone would have been unthinkable without air superiority.

At 1610hrs, the IDF ordered the IAF to widen the scope of air support through attacks against Jordanian armor in the Samaria sector. Three minutes later, two Squadron 119 Mirages departed Ekron to photograph, from high altitude, the JAF bases of Amman and Mafraq, as well as the SAF bases at Baly, Mazzeh, Dumayr, and Saikal. No enemy aircraft – Iraqi, JAF, or SAF, let alone the EAF, which did not penetrate Israel's airspace at all during Day 1 – flew offensive operations over Israel after about 1430hrs. The JAF had been wiped out but the SAF had been only halved in strength, so Syrian defensive operations could not be ruled out. Therefore, at 1615hrs, two Squadron 101 Mirages were scrambled from Khatsor to escort the unarmed Squadron 119 reconnaissance Mirages.

At 1625hrs, Command South reported to the IDF that Locality Oakland had been occupied, thus rendering the airdrop part of Operation *Nachshons 80* unnecessary.

At 1631hrs, the scope of the IAF's support role was widened when Mission 107/14 departed Lod tasked to attack Jordanian armor in the Samaria sector. Until that time IAF support was limited to the IDF Command South theater of operations, even though Command Center and Command North had been fighting Jordanian forces in Samaria and Judea since noon. According to primary sources available at the time of writing, it seems that both Command Center and Command North waited patiently for *Focus* to conclude and did not forward requests for air support; the initiation of IAF support missions over Command Center and Command North theaters of operation was at the initiative of the IDF rather than as a result of requests from Command Center or Command North.

A BDA image of Dumayr looking northwest on the threshold of runway 24. Five bomb craters are clearly visible on the runway, plus one near miss, and two craters placed right on the parallel taxiway. Three black stains over the two visible aprons may well have been burned-out combat aircraft. Squadron 119 pilots Uri Yaari and Reuben Rosen flew a high-altitude reconnaissance mission over Amman, Mafraq, Baly, Mazzeh, Dumayr, and Saikal from 1613 to 1700hrs. (AC)

Finally, after a 56-minute break with no IAF departures tasked to strike enemy air bases, the first *Focus* fifth-wave mission, Mission 105/26, departed Khatsor tasked to bomb – just bomb – Inchas aiming point 1 along runway 04/22 with two 250kg bombs per Super Mystère. KNESSET faced intense antiaircraft fire, spotted ongoing repair work along runway 04/22, and reported that all four Super Mystères hit the allocated target. KNESSET had been ordered not to strafe Inchas but seems to have added a personal touch to the interpretation of this order. During egress, the Super Mystères instead strafed Bilbeis, where an Il-14 was claimed as destroyed, as well as targets of opportunity: two trucks at an unspecified location, a radar station near Ismailia, and a railway station near Bardavil.

Four formations followed from 1637 to 1649hrs, tasked to bomb runways at Fayid, Bir Gafgafa, Inchas again, and Cairo International. Then, at 1650hrs, Squadron 110's KISHON departed Ramat David to strike Ras Banas, adjacent to the coast of the Red Sea, some 970km along a straight line from Ramat David. Two Squadron 110 Vautour formations were planned to strike Ras Banas in the original March 16 *Focus A* task assignment program when AIR4 evaluated that a Tu-16 flight would detach to Ras Banas in line with the EAF emergency deployment plan. AIR3 dropped Ras Banas from the updated *Focus A* task assignment program that was issued on May 23, while AIR4 did not report any aircraft based at Ras Banas on the morning of June 5. Yet KISHON was tasked to strike Ras Banas, the longest-range IAF fighter force mission during the Six-Day War. Postwar, IAF Commander Moti Hod explained:

There were six [Egyptian] Il-28s in Yemen and we received a message that they departed [Yemen] back to Egypt. We rushed and bombed Ras Banas because we evaluated that if Ras Banas [was] closed then they would have no other place to land for fuel… We told the pilots to bomb the runway and if there [were] aircraft [there then] to attack [the parked aircraft]… We figured that if they had landed then we would attack them on the ground or [if they had not landed yet] close the field and they would have nowhere to fly to.

The KISHON aircraft were all single-seat Vautour IIA, because the Vautour IIB had no cannon and the Vautour IIN had less fuel. At the time flying as KISHON 1, Isaac Golan recalled:

> The target was at the limit of our high-altitude radius of action. We flew a long time, more than an hour in each direction, the most economical flight possible, climbing higher as fuel was consumed and weight went down. We got to Ras Banas and nothing was there, nothing at all, not a single aircraft to strafe. We bombed the runway and returned.

Had the Egyptian Il-28s already landed and departed? Or not arrived yet? It has been claimed that the six Il-28s landed at Cairo International Airport at around 1600hrs, but Squadron 101's COUNTER – which bombed Cairo International at around 1720hrs and provided a relatively detailed debrief – did not report Il-28s on the ground at Cairo International, and neither did Squadron 119's APARTMENT and DOOR that also bombed Cairo International around 1740hrs and 1820hrs, respectively. Postwar, IAF Commander Moti Hod summed up:

> The six [Egyptian Il-28] bombers indeed arrived at Ras Banas [but were unable to land there because of damage to the runway so] they turned [and flew on] to Mecca [in Saudi Arabia] and somehow they got to Mecca but [then] instead of returning to Egypt they returned to Yemen.

Meanwhile, at 1700hrs, according to Arab sources, Syria exploited a break in IAF missions striking SAF bases to announce the shooting down of 50 Israeli aircraft, an over-claim of 700 percent which seems to have been the standard over-claim for Egypt, Iraq, and Syria that day.

Either way, from 1701 to 1800hrs, the IAF dispatched ten missions tasked to bomb seven Egyptian airfields – Abu Sueir, Bir Gafgafa, Bir Tamada, Cairo International, Cairo West, Fayid, and Kabrit – plus three missions to strike SAF base Dumayr. None of the IAF *Focus* fifth-wave formations encountered enemy aircraft in the air; the only combat aircraft flying over the theater of operations at that time were Israeli. The IAF accomplished air superiority and was gearing up to initiate full exploitation of that superiority from the morning of Day 2, even though air support operations were stepped up during the fifth wave (IAF combat aircraft departures from 1600 to 1840hrs inclusive).

Focus fifth-wave missions, sorties, air-to-air kills, and losses[1]							
Squadron	Patrol missions/ sorties	SEAB[2] missions/ sorties	Support missions/ sorties	Other missions/ sorties	Total	Kills[3]	Losses
101 Mirage	5/10	2/7	-/-	1/2[4]	8/19	-	-
105 Super Mystère	-/-	5/19	1/3	2/4[5]	8/26	-	-
107 Ouragan	-/-	-/-	4/8	-/-	4/8	-	-
109 Mystère	-/-	2/8	1/2	-/-	3/10	-	-
110 Vautour	-/-	3/11	-/-	-/-	3/11	-	-
113 Ouragan	-/-	2/8	3/10	-/-	5/18	-	-
116 Mystère	-/-	1/2	-/-	-/-	1/2	-	-
117 Mirage	4/8	2/6	-/-	-/-	6/14	-	-
119 Mirage	1/2	2/6	-/-	1/2[6]	4/10	-	-
147 Fouga	-/-	-/-	7/23	1/1[7]	8/24	-	1
Total	10/20	19/67	16/46	5/9	50/142	-	1

The final *Focus* mission tasked to strike an enemy air base during Day 1 of the hostilities departed Ramat David at 1800hrs tasked to bomb Abu Sueir, and returned to Ramat David at 1900hrs, some 20 minutes past sunset at 1840hrs, at which point we draw the line to end the *Focus* fifth wave. From the first takeoff at 0714hrs to the last landing at 1900hrs, *Focus* was finished almost within 12 hours.

Squadron 110's NIGER departed Ramat David at 1731hrs to strike Bir Tamada. The three Vautours bombed the runway and then split up. NIGER 1 – flying a reconnaissance Vautour IIB – photographed roads in Sinai from low altitude, and near Mount Libni it photographed the Il-14 that Squadron 101's SOFA 2 had shot down nine hours earlier. NIGER 2 and 3 strafed tents and vehicles southwest of Mount Hillal and claimed destruction of five to ten trucks. (AC)

ANALYSIS AND AFTERMATH

Focus in figures

Since the first air superiority campaign against an enemy with an integrated air defense system to shield its air assets – which was fought over southern England in summer 1940 – no other such campaign has achieved air superiority as rapidly and unambiguously as *Focus*. Within 12 hours, a force of less than 200 combat aircraft flew nearly 700 sorties, raided 26 enemy airfields in four nations, and claimed the destruction on the ground and in the air of more than 400 aircraft, for the loss of only 24 aircraft, giving an unprecedented claim-to-loss ratio of nearly 20 to one.

Compared with *Focus*, the German air superiority campaign of the Battle of Britain was fought between roughly equal-sized opponents, lasted over three months, targeted many irrelevant targets, was conducted almost at leisure, and yielded claim-to-loss ratios that were rarely better than one to one.

Compared with other air superiority campaigns, *Focus* was exceptionally successful in three principal areas:

- It was achieved despite the initial balance of power being distinctly in favor of the defending force, whereas, in most modern warfare air superiority campaigns, the defending force was significantly smaller than the offensive force.
- The timeframe of the campaign lasted mere hours and focused on the destruction of combat aircraft on the ground, whereas most modern warfare air superiority campaigns lasted days, weeks, and months with targeting of assets such as radar stations and airfield facilities that have little significance without combat aircraft to support.
- The campaign swung the balance of power; the concluding balance of power differed dramatically from the initial one.

Narratives striving to present an Arab perspective or even a "balanced" view consistently suggest that IAF claims were either exaggerated in good faith and/or intentionally inflated.

However, it should be remembered that Israeli aircrews' claims were made during a few hours when the accuracy of reports was known to be crucial to the success of the campaign – and, arguably, national survival. In the IDF Officers' School, it is stressed time and again that a successful military organization cannot exist without credibility along the chain of command.

Obviously, reports from field commanders are the basis for planning by staff officers. In the case of *Focus*, AIR4 collected debriefs from squadrons, fused and meshed information from debriefs with data collected from other intelligence sources such as listening, monitoring, observation, and photography, processed the raw data together with AIR2 experts, and streamed the output to AIR3 so that AIR3 would prepare an optimal plan for fighting and issue corresponding mission orders back to the squadrons. Credible reports were therefore, supposedly, in the interest of the reporting field units. Still, ambitiousness and optimism are human traits, so within any organization some exaggerated claims seem inevitable. It was therefore the task of AIR4 to process the data and to produce realistic assessments for decision-makers. The IAF embraced this policy and, for example, reported to the IDF at 0920hrs that 150 EAF aircraft had been destroyed, a cautious and conservative number well below the accumulated number of claims.

Yet, in comparison with other air campaigns, *Focus* claims seem to be less exaggerated and more credible. The Battle of Britain saw a 300 percent over-claim rate, and the Egyptian and Syrian official statements on June 5, 1967, a 700 percent over-claim rate – albeit the latter claim was chiefly for propaganda purposes. The accuracy was perhaps due both to the very limited timeframe of *Focus* and the importance of victory, which allowed less room for self-interest, as well as the quality of IAF training and command.

So how many EAF, Iraqi, JAF, and SAF aircraft were destroyed during *Focus*? While IAF losses and claims are mostly generated from Israeli primary sources – debriefs, logs, and reports – there are no equivalent Egyptian, Iraqi, Jordanian, and Syrian primary sources. Therefore, the number of IAF losses is accurate while the number of EAF, Iraqi, JAF, and SAF losses is not known for sure.

Focus sorties and claims									
	Sorties[1]	Destructions[2]							
		MiG-15/17	MiG-19	MiG-21	Su-7	Hunter	Il-28	Tu-16	Others[3]
Egypt El Arish	8	7	–	–	–	–	–	–	1
Egypt Jabel Libni	10	4	–	–	–	–	–	–	–
Egypt Bir Tamada	25	10	–	–	–	–	–	–	6
Egypt Bir Gafgafa	30	–	–	10	–	–	–	–	9
Egypt Abu Sueir	52	4	–	11		–	22	–	1
Egypt Fayid	50	8	–	22	1	–	–	–	2
Egypt Kabrit	40	33	–	–	–	–	–	–	1
Egypt Bilbeis	12	–	–	–	–	–	–	–	8
Egypt Cairo International	10	–	–	1	–	–	–	–	–
Egypt Cairo West	37	13	1	10	–	–	5	11	1
Egypt Helwan	4	2	1	–	–	–	–	–	3

	Sorties[1]	Destructions[2]							
		MiG-15/17	MiG-19	MiG-21	Su-7	Hunter	Il-28	Tu-16	Others[3]
Egypt Inchas	33	7	–	21	–	–	–	–	1
Egypt Mansura	12	–	–	2	–	–	–	–	–
Egypt Minya	8	–	–	–	–	–	–	–	8
Egypt Beni Suef	10	–	–	–	–	–	–	10	–
Egypt Hurghada	4	1	5	–	–	–	–	–	3
Egypt Luxor	3	–	–	–	–	–	–	5	10
Egypt Ras Banas	4	–	–	–	–	–	–	–	–
Iraq H-3	3	–	–	6	–	3	–	–	1
Jordan Amman	24	–	–	–	–	3	–	–	9
Jordan Mafraq	24	–	–	–	–	16	–	–	–
Syria Baly	12	10	–	–	–	–	–	–	1
Syria Dumayr	22	4	3[4]	9	–	–	–	–	–
Syria Mazzeh	14	7	–	–	–	–	2	–	4
Syria Saikal	12	2	–	2	–	–	–	–	–
Syria T-4	7	3	–	5	–	–	–	–	1
Total destructions on the ground	–	115	10	99	1	22	29	26[5]	70
Total credited air-to-air kills	–	6	3	11	-	3	-	-	3
Initial inventory Egypt	–	96	28	102	16	–	27	30	–
Initial inventory Iraq	–	30	–	32	–	48	11	10	–
Initial inventory Jordan	–	–	–	–	–	24	–	–	–
Initial inventory Syria	–	35	–	60	–	–	2	–	–
Overall destruction[6]	–	75%	46%	57%	6%	35%	72%	65%	–

Notes:

1 AIR1 Statistics, not necessarily 100 percent accurate but certainly almost 100 percent accurate. Total number of missions was 470.

2 AIR1 History

3 An-12, Il-14, Mi-4, Mi-6 etc

4 The SAF is not known to have operated the MiG-19, possibly misidentification

5 The IAF concluded that all EAF Tu-16s had been destroyed and therefore "rounded" the claim to 30

6 Overall, the IAF claimed destruction of 57 percent of EAF, Iraqi, JAF, and SAF combat aircraft

Arguably, more important than the numbers of aircraft destroyed are the numbers either destroyed or damaged. For the objectives that the IAF set, an EAF combat aircraft that was damaged during a *Focus* mission and only repaired after the war was as good as a destroyed aircraft. So how did *Focus* affect EAF, JAF, SAF, and Iraqi operations? The impact was devastating. Assuming a rather low figure of 66 percent serviceability and a quite modest exploitation of two sorties per combat aircraft per 24 hours, the Egyptian, Iraqi, Jordanian, and Syrian air forces should have been able to project around 400, 200, 30, and 130 sorties respectively per 24 hours, or a total of 760 sorties per 24 hours from a nominal force of around 570 combat aircraft. During June 5, 1967, the IAF counted only 51 EAF combat aircraft sorties, of which none was offensive, and only 74 SAF combat aircraft sorties, of which just 12 were offensive. The EAF and SAF therefore exploited less than 13 percent and 57 percent respectively of their actual combat potential during the crucial first day of the war, while most of the SAF sorties had been flown prior to IAF missions to strike SAF bases. Similarly, Iraq and the JAF flew offensive operations against Israel only until the IAF raided H-3, Amman, and Mafraq, when Iraqi and JAF offensive operations practically ceased until the end of Day 1 of the war.

Air support

Initially, the IDF planned an evening H-Hour for a ground offensive against Egypt in order to penetrate their front-line Sinai fortifications during nighttime and the next morning begin to destroy the Egyptian armor that was deployed behind them. But Operation *Focus* was deemed so important that the IDF had to conform to the IAF H-Hour. The partial solution was to assign Squadron 147 Fouga armed trainers to support IDF Command South's offensive pending the conclusion of *Focus*. The revised IDF plans for Day 1 of the war were:

IDF Chief of Staff Isaac Rabin and IAF Commander Moti Hod attended a media conference from 1855hrs on June 7, 1967, during which the latter presented the highlights of IAF accomplishments up to that point. (ILGP/PO)

- Command South was tasked to penetrate Sinai through the Egyptian front-line fortifications with minimum support from the IAF.
- Command Center and Command North were tasked to hold positions against Jordan and Syria, respectively, in the hope that neither would join hostilities.
- The IAF was tasked to accomplish air superiority through the destruction on the ground of EAF combat aircraft.

The success of *Focus* enabled the IAF to begin to send combat aircraft to support Command South much sooner than expected. However, Jordan and Syria then joined hostilities, and IDF plans were updated accordingly:

- Command South was tasked to press ahead with the penetration into Sinai with minimum support from the IAF.
- Command Center and Command North were tasked to push back Jordanian artillery that from around 1140hrs had been bombarding IAF bases – and other targets within Israel – with minimum support from the IAF.
- Command North was tasked to hold positions against Syria.
- The IAF was tasked to achieve air superiority through the destruction on the ground of JAF and SAF combat aircraft.

By the end of the first day – sunset on June 5 was at 1840hrs – the IAF had air superiority and had become the largest and most powerful air force among the combatant nations, with an operational inventory of up to 180 combat aircraft that were capable of generating up to 900 sorties per day. The residual force of the EAF, JAF, and SAF – with generous allowance for potential IAF over-claiming of destruction – could hardly have been expected to be as much as 150 sorties per day, and in reality was less than half that number. Obviously, Arab expeditionary forces – especially combat aircraft from Algeria and Iraq – could have been expected to be deployed to Egypt, Jordan, and Syria, hence Israel's application of David Ben-Gurion's defense doctrine: fight on the enemy's soil a short war with unambiguous outcome.

Despite the IDF's limited expectations, the IAF flew 268 support sorties by the end of Day 1 out of a reported total 857 fighter force sorties. Most support missions during that day were relatively close to the front line – not more than 10km deep – and mostly targeted armor, artillery, and fortifications. For example, Squadron 147 reported 173 sorties – including 16 tasked to strike radars in support of Operation *Focus* – and the destruction of 40 tanks, 19 armored vehicles, 52 trucks, 38 artillery pieces, two trains, and four antiaircraft guns, plus static targets such as fortifications and logistics centers. Reported destructions were obviously the upper limit because not all hits resulted in destruction; because sometimes an already-destroyed target was claimed as destroyed again; and because near misses could look like a hit. Still, the tally even on Day 1 was significant and certainly had an impact upon the conduct of war. From the second day, the impact was more significant.

The other five days

From the second day of the war, June 6, the IAF repulsed IDF pressure to continue SEAB missions. The IAF logic was that the residual Arab air power should be met in the air rather than risk IAF aircraft in strike missions against heavily defended and now forewarned targets. Thus from Day 2 the IAF fighter force mostly supported the IDF, but also flew patrols to defend the IDF from Arab air strikes. IAF Day 2 statistics indicated it flew 614 support sorties out of 734 total fighter force sorties. AIR4 monitoring during June 6 recorded only 67 Egyptian combat aircraft sorties and just six Syrian combat aircraft sorties. The impact of air superiority was evident, as was the IAF dictum to meet residual Arab air power in the air. The IAF credited 14 air-to-air kills during Day 2, plus one ground-to-air kill, making the approximate Egyptian and Syrian loss ratio a staggering 21 percent, according to AIR4 data.

IAF air superiority enabled the IDF to operate without fear of Arab air strikes and to destroy the Egyptian forces in Sinai and Jordanian forces in Judea and Samaria, while

A Squadron 110 Vautour photographing retreating Egyptian forces in Sinai on June 7 or 8, 1967. (AC)

simultaneously holding off Syria. The combined pressure of the IDF and IAF crumbled the Egyptian and Jordanian deployments to the point that both forces were ordered to retreat. IDF Intelligence indicated at 1325hrs on June 6 that the Jordanian forces in Judea and Samaria had been ordered to retreat to the East Bank of the River Jordan. At 0410hrs on June 7, IDF Intelligence reported that the Egyptian retreat from Sinai had begun at 0300hrs.

IAF operations against retreating forces without air cover were obviously devastating. At around 2000hrs on June 7, the Jordanian Brigade 40 completed its retreat from Samaria with only eight tanks left out of an initial inventory of around 100. The Jordanians attributed the lion's share of their losses to IAF air strikes. Likewise, the IDF evaluated that Egypt deployed to Sinai 100,000 troops and 1,000 tanks. Again, this was probably an upper-boundary estimate, as prewar IDF Intelligence evaluations set the number of Egyptian tanks in Sinai at variously 801, 810–20, or 914. Either way, the Egyptian retreat from Sinai safeguarded roughly half of the equipment – and more than half of the troops – so some 500 Egyptian tanks were left behind in Sinai, with about half of those destroyed and half damaged or intact.

By the end of Day 4 (June 8), the IDF was completing the occupation of Sinai and the conquest of Judea and Samaria from Jordan. During Day 5 and Day 6 (June 9–10), the IDF took and occupied the Golan Heights from Syria, with the IAF flying 644 support sorties to attack Syrian targets, against only 28 support sorties to attack Egyptian forces during this timeframe, and out of 877 IAF fighter force sorties flown during these last two days of the Six-Day War.

IAF AIR1 reported 3,718 fighter force sorties from June 5 to 10, including 2,591 support sorties. IAF AIR4 monitored only 365 Egyptian and Syrian combat aircraft sorties during that timeframe.

The IAF lost 46 aircraft from June 5 to 10: ten Ouragans, nine Mirages, nine Super Mystères, seven Mystères, six Fougas, four Vautours, and one Nord. IAF AIR1 Statistics claimed the destruction of:

•   452 enemy aircraft on the ground and in the air.

- 545 tanks, including 338 Egyptian, 150 Jordanian, and 57 Syrian.
- 227 armored vehicles, including 147 Egyptian, 69 Jordanian, and 11 Syrian.
- 1,326 vehicles, including 753 Egyptian, 423 Jordanian, and 150 Syrian.

Again, these figures should be treated as an upper limit. For example, the IDF reported that Egypt lost 509 tanks, Jordan 179 and Syria 118;[15] on July 16 the IDF Armor Corps Commander retorted that IAF data should be referred to as attacks from the air rather than actual destructions. On July 24, the IAF Commander reluctantly agreed to the semantics suggested by the IDF Armor Corps Commander.

A further tool to evaluate the effectiveness of IAF Six-Day War support missions is the results of friendly fire incidents. The IDF reported 14 friendly fire air-strike incidents, during which 44 IAF fighter force sorties attacked IDF units; attacks that resulted in 12 troops killed, 59 injured, 13 damaged/destroyed tanks, eight damaged/destroyed armored vehicles, and five damaged/destroyed other vehicles. A simple extrapolation from these 44 sorties to the 965 support missions flown over Sinai suggests that the IAF upper-boundary claim is not a far-fetched figure and may well be a very realistic report. The friendly fire incidents also only involved attacks against fighting forces, whereas many, if not the majority, of IAF support sorties were against logistics echelons, which were generally softer targets.

These three sets of figures – IAF sorties against EAF and SAF sorties, IAF losses against claims, and IAF support statistics – all demonstrate that the impact of IAF air superiority upon the conduct of the Six-Day War was indeed overwhelming.

15   These numbers are most likely absolutely correct since most if not all of the tanks that Egypt, Jordan, and Syria lost during the war remained in the areas that the IDF occupied.

IAF air superiority allowed it to fly devastating air support missions, especially against enemy units moving on roads during daylight, as this image of abandoned and destroyed Egyptian vehicles on a road in Sinai, photographed from an IAF Piper, clearly illustrates. It enabled the IDF to occupy the Sinai Peninsula within four days, Judea and Samaria within three days, and the Golan Heights within two days. (AC)

BIBLIOGRAPHY AND FURTHER READING

Writing about the past is a dynamic process. The past is described through sources that are available at present, but additional sources may surface in the future and may change the then present perspective of the past.

This text is mostly based upon Israeli primary sources: intelligence reports, operational orders, mission orders, formation debriefs, and unit logs. These primary sources are often compared with the IAF's postwar AIR1 Statistics and AIR1 History, as well as – to a lesser extent – with narratives such as *Arab MiGs* that attempt to present an Arab perspective.

There are no known primary sources from the Arab side, except for a number of documents – primarily the EAF from the prewar period – that the IDF captured and released.[16] In any case, this text is presented from the perspective of *Focus*. Whenever possible, the data and information that was available to the IDF and IAF at the time of the events is compared with recent revelations about what happened, but what mattered to the actual conduct of *Focus* was the data and information that was available to the IDF and IAF at the time of the events.

A small selection of recollections was added to enliven and enrich the factual text, but readers are advised to refer to memories in a critical manner. Many more recollections can be found in the books in the bibliography. Memoirs and recollections are often invaluable to support primary sources, but rarely as standalone sources. Again, readers are advised to refer to memoirs and recollections as secondary sources.

Aloni, Shlomo, *Israeli Air Force Air Campaigns: The June 1967 Six-Day War Volume A: Operation Focus The Israeli Pre-Emptive Strike Of June 5, 1967*, Isradecal, Israel (2008)

Aloni, Shlomo, *Mirage III Vs MiG-21: Six-Day War 1967*, Osprey Duel 28, Oxford (2010)

Aloni, Shlomo, *Vultures Over Israel: The Vautour in Israeli Service: Squadron 110 1957–1971*, Schiffer Publishing, Atglen, Pennsylvania (2011)

Aloni, Shlomo, *Jezreel Valley Mystères: The Mystère IVa In Israeli Air Force Service: Squadron 109 1956–1968*, Schiffer Publishing, Atglen, Pennsylvania (2015)

Cooper, Tom, *Arab MiGs Volume 2: Supersonic Fighters, 1958–1967*, Harpia Publishing (2011)

Cooper, Tom, *Arab MiGs Volume 3: The June 1967 War*, Harpia Publishing (2012)

Cooper, Tom, *Hawker Hunters At War, Iraq And Jordan, 1958–1967*, Helion, Solihull, West Midlands (2016)

Ginor, Isabella and Remez Gideon, *Foxbats Over Dimona, The Soviets' Nuclear Gamble in the Six-Day War*, Yale University Press, New Haven, Connecticut (2007)

---

16   The documents were captured in EAF bases in Sinai. The IDF initially released – in June 1967, a short while after the end of the war – a small selection of those documents – with the original in Arabic, plus translation to English – in order to prove to the world that the EAF prepared offensive operation orders aimed at attacking Israel.

Gordon, Yefim and Komissarov, Dmitriy, *Soviet and Russian Military Aircraft in The Middle East*, Hikoki Publications, Manchester (2013)

Nicolle, David, *Arab MiG-19 And MiG-21 Units in Combat*, Osprey Combat Aircraft 44, Oxford (2004)

Nordeen, Lon and Nicolle, David, *Phoenix over the Nile A History of Egyptian Air Power 1932–1994*, Smithsonian Institution Press, Washington DC, 1996

INDEX